PRAISE FOR

*A Trustworthy Anchor:
God's Hope & Encouragement in the Storms of Life*

I highly recommend Shirley Mozena's wonderful book, *A Trustworthy Anchor: God's Hope & Encouragement in the Storms of Life*. Shirley writes in a genuine way that reaches your soul with deep truth and compassionate love. You will be touched and forever changed by her gentle yet straight-to-the-heart real life stories! Pick up this book and you will immediately get lost in its pages, seeing yourself in each story! Be encouraged and inspired by this amazing book!

~William J. Federer
nationally known speaker, best-selling author of books on American history, politics, and culture, as well as president of Amerisearch, Inc. (americanminute.com)

I love the name of Shirley Mozena's new devotional book: *A Trustworthy Anchor: God's Hope & Encouragement in the Storms of Life*. Shirley has experienced significant loss and has trusted God as an anchor through it all. Her writing flows from her everyday life and the experiences that have shaped a sound faith anchored deeply in the love and compassion of a faithful God. Shirley takes those experiences and shares them in a way that allows us to know that God is present in the storms of life and He remains the anchor that provides the hope and encouragement that we all desperately need. Shirley has a unique ability to take the truth of Scripture and apply it to daily life, especially when daily life is in the midst of a personal storm. Whether you are currently in a storm, or one is around the corner, this book will empower you to see God's face and trust Him to see you through to the other side. I highly recommend this book and I believe you will be the better for having read its wisdom.

~Rich Blum
Senior Pastor, Bethel Community Church, Washougal, Washington
(bethelcommunitychurch.org)

When we've been tossed about by the storms of life, God's Word moors us to His presence and peace. In *A Trustworthy Anchor*, Shirley Quiring Mozena invites readers to pull into a safe harbor with God in the midst of life's troubles. Each devotion draws in the reader with a well-crafted story that illustrates the spiritual principle found in the daily Bible verse. Mozena also offers wisdom gained over her lifetime anchored to God and provides the opportunity to reflect on personal application. You'll want to return to this wonderful resource again and again.

~Annie Yorty
Author, *From Ignorance to Bliss: God's Heart Revealed through Down Syndrome* and *Find Jesus in 25 Symbols of Christmas—A Devotional* (annieyorty.com)

The inescapable nature of life is that it comes with storms. They can't be avoided, no matter how carefully we plan, prepare and set up protective walls. Sometimes they arrive quietly, like a light, summer shower, causing us only to pause and reassess. Other times they arrive in a rage, a merciless cyclone of destruction, requiring complete restructuring. What we need to be convinced of, is the truth that God is with you in *every single storm*. And that's what *A Trustworthy Anchor* provides through scripture and story - proof that God is in the storm with you and knows the way out. This devotional is the resource to keep at your fingertips for when those storm clouds start to gather.

~Janice Mayo Mathers
Board Chair, Stonecroft Ministries and author of Stonecroft Bible Study,
Every Season - Embracing Your Forever Purpose

A TRUSTWORTHY
Anchor

A TRUSTWORTHY
Anchor

GOD'S HOPE & ENCOURAGEMENT
IN THE STORMS OF LIFE

A FORTY-DAY DEVOTIONAL

SHIRLEY QUIRING MOZENA

SCM
PUBLISHING

© 2024 by Shirley Quiring Mozena. All rights reserved.

Noncommercial interests may reproduce portions of this book without the express written permission of the author, provided the text does not exceed five hundred words. When reproducing text from this book, include the following credit line: "A Trustworthy Anchor: God's Hope & Encouragement in the Storms of Life by Shirley Quiring Mozena. Used by permission."

Commercial interests: No part of this publication may be reproduced in any form, stored in a retrieval system, or transmitted in any form by any means—electronic, photocopy, recording, or otherwise—without prior written permission of the publisher/author, except as provided by United States of America copyright law.

All Scripture quotations, unless otherwise indicated, are taken from the Holy Bible, New International Version®, NIV®. Copyright ©1973, 1978, 1984, 2011 by Biblica, Inc.® Used by permission of Zondervan. All rights reserved worldwide. www.zondervan.com. The "NIV" and "New International Version" are trademarks registered in the United States Patent and Trademark Office by Biblica, Inc.®

Scripture quotations marked (NLT) are taken from the Holy Bible, New Living Translation, copyright ©1996, 2004, 2015 by Tyndale House Foundation. Used by permission of Tyndale House Publishers, a Division of Tyndale House Ministries, Carol Stream, Illinois 60188. All rights reserved.

Scripture quotations Marked (ESV) are from the ESV® Bible (The Holy Bible, English Standard Version®), © 2001 by Crossway, a publishing ministry of Good News Publishers. Used by permission. All rights reserved. The ESV text may not be quoted in any publication made available to the public by a Creative Commons license. The ESV may not be translated in whole or in part into any other language.

Scripture quotations marked (NCV) are taken from the New Century Version®. Copyright © 2005 by Thomas Nelson. Used by permission. All rights reserved.

Scripture quotations marked (NET) are from the NET Bible® copyright ©1996, 2019 by Biblical Studies Press, L.L.C. http://netbible.com. Used by permission. All rights reserved.

Scripture quotations marked (NMB) are from the New Matthew Bible, Copyright © 2016 by Ruth Magnusson (Davis). Includes emendations to February 2022. All rights reserved.

Scripture quotations marked (PHILLIPS) are from the New Testament in Modern English by J. B. Phillips copyright © 1960, 1972 J. B. Phillips. Administered by The Archbishops' Council of the Church of England. Used by Permission.

Scripture quotations marked (HCSB) are taken from the Holman Christian Standard Bible®, Copyright © 1999, 2000, 2002, 2003, 2009 by Holman Bible Publishers. Used by permission. Holman Christian Standard Bible®, Holman CSB®, and HCSB® are federally registered trademarks of Holman Bible Publishers.

Scripture quotations marked (GNT) are from the Good News Translation in Today's English Version-Second Edition Copyright © 1992 by American Bible Society. Used by Permission.

ISBN: 979-8-9891355-6-1

Library of Congress Catalog Card Number: 2024913037

I dedicate this book to Jesus Christ, the author and finisher of my faith. He was there before there was time. I've found him to be a trustworthy anchor in my life during both the calm times and storms in my life. I'm grateful for every circumstance God used to draw me into the beauty, tumult, and adventures he allowed that caused me to enter the "curtain of God's inner sanctuary."

"This hope is a strong and trustworthy anchor for our souls. It leads us through the curtain into God's inner sanctuary" (Hebrews 6:19 NLT).

Contents

Introduction 1
The Voice 7
Tenacious Love 11
Even When Afraid, I Will Trust 15
Unfamiliar Paths 17
Remembering to Rest 21
Surprised by Joy 23
Who Was He? 25
What is it to Ponder? 29
How About a Spiritual Diet? 31
A New Heart 35
The Tale of a Baseball Mitt 39
This Old House 43
Safety Under the Feathers 49
We Learn to Become One 53
Entertaining Angels 57
Renewed Strength 59
The Scent of the Master 61
Broken Hearts to Mend 63

Nothing Can Separate 65
Facing Absence 69
We Have Hope 73
The Dance of a Lifetime... 75
Table for One 79
A Cheerful Robin...81
No Timetable for Grief... 83
Grief with Hope 87
Take Your Time... 89
All Will Be Well... 93
Forever Peace 99
A Sacred Cloakroom 103
He Knows Us 105
Things Can Change...107
Unexpected Protection from God 111
The Dawn Reveals...113
The Bread of Life..115
Someone Safe, Someone Good 117
Give the Blessing 119
Want to Meet for Coffee?... 123
We're Standing on Their Shoulders 127
Look to the East 129

Endnotes.. 131
Acknowledgments... 133
About the Author... 135
Other Books by Shirley 137

Introduction

May the God of hope fill you with all joy and peace as you trust in him, so that you may overflow with hope by the power of the Holy Spirit.
—Romans 15:13

Romans 15:13 inspired me more than a decade ago. Within four short years, I had lost two husbands to death. I never believed I'd love anyone like I loved my first husband, Bill, but I was surprised.

Two years after losing Bill, I married Blair, and we delighted in each other and our second chance at love. I expected many years with this man; but it was not to be, for only seventeen months after our wedding, he died suddenly.

I disliked being alone. I didn't like being a widow. And honestly, I felt cheated. Memories of my life with each husband comforted me, but the days and nights dragged on, day after day, night after night. There wasn't anything tangible I could latch on to but hope in those days. Hope that I wouldn't feel so lonely, so lost. As I coped through the nights, longing for sleep when it wouldn't come, I placed my hope in Jesus Christ. Although I had trusted in Jesus for my salvation many years earlier, my relationship became even closer and more intimate during those many months. He was the calm in my storm. An anchor. I'm reminded of an old hymn that tells us to hold fast:

> *We have an anchor that keeps the soul*
> *Steadfast and sure while the billows roll,*
> *Fastened to the Rock which cannot move,*
> *Grounded firm and deep in the Savior's love.*
> —"We Have an Anchor" by Priscilla J. Owens, 1829–1907[1]

During the storms in your life, I can tell you of an anchor on which you can rely. That anchor will keep you "steadfast and sure." It is Jesus Christ, the One who died for you and then rose from death. He promises eternal life with him when you acknowledge your sin and believe he did these things for you.

While grieving my husbands, I attempted to read fiction to escape the reality of my loss, but I could not. Yet I could always—even in deep grief—meditate on God's Word. It was my anchor then and continues to be now. "We Have an Anchor" is based on these words from the New Testament: "This hope is a strong and trustworthy anchor for our souls. It leads us through the curtain into God's inner sanctuary" (Hebrews 6:19 NLT). God worked the days of my being alone into a good thing for me. I entered through the curtain of God's inner sanctuary a place I may not have experienced without those deaths.

I learned to be content in the state of singleness, and at just the right time God brought a wonderful man, Jim, into my life. We married ten years ago and together have leaned in on the truth of Scripture and grown spiritually. We understand how second chances—whether it is reconnecting with God, an improved marriage, or even finding love again—are totally the work of our Creator. My husband Jim and I have experienced great joy in finding each other.

> *Trust him in the common light;*
> *Trust him in the awesome night;*

> *Trust him when the earth doth quake:*
> *Trust him when thy heart doth ache;*
> *Trust him when thy brain doth reel*
> *And thy friend turns on his heel;*
> *Trust him when the way is rough,*
> *Cry not yet, "It is enough!"*
> *But obey with true endeavor,*
> *Else the salt hath lost his savor.*
> —"Obedience" by George MacDonald[2]

What a promise God gives us to be our anchor. A trustworthy one. I've been praying for you, my dear reader, that you will experience God's hope, comfort, and truth through the storms in your life. If you are not in a storm right now, this state of calm is your time to envelop yourself in God's promises through his Word. Then when the storm comes, you'll be fully anchored and grounded in the Savior's love. That's when the anchor digs deeper and keeps you steady. There is hope in the promise from the prophet, "For I know the plans I have for you, declares the LORD, plans for welfare and not for evil, to give you a future and a hope" (Jeremiah 29:11 ESV). What hope that God has a plan for each one of us who put our faith and trust in Him. A plan for good and not evil. To give a future and a hope.

It is my prayer that the meditations that follow coupled with my short stories will inspire you to read further in the precious love letter from God, the Bible. In the inspired words, you will find hope, promise, encouragement, comfort, and truth for your life. Grasp on to the truth of God's Word. Study it. Ask God to reveal what he would have you learn from his Word. Take this time—whether you are in a storm or not—to read and consider words that will encourage, build your faith, and bring joy. Trust the Anchor.

Part I

Anchored in
Hope

The Voice

*My sheep listen to my voice; I know them, and they follow me.
I give them eternal life, and they shall never perish;
no one will snatch them out of my hand.
My Father, who has given them to me, is greater than all;
no one can snatch them out of my Father's hand.
I and the Father are one.*
—John 10:27–30

"Tell me the story of when you and Uncle Arnie got lost in the snowstorm," I begged as my mother and I picked berries in the hot summer sun. She grew up in northeastern Montana where the winters are fierce and cruel, and the time went so much faster when she was telling a story. She was the best storyteller. Leaning into the strawberry bushes, she began.

>The teacher dismissed us from school early because there were storm warnings. It had begun to snow, and the wind picked up. We walked along the fence line, so we had a guide to stay out of the ditch.

The wind was as noisy as a freight train on the railroad tracks that whizzed by our farm each afternoon. Wanting to get home, we took the shortcut across the field. In the big empty space, with no fence line for reference, we stumbled through snowdrifts. The snow was so blinding, like Mama's starched white sheets hung out on the line to dry—nothing but white. We remembered what our parents told us: *Always hold hands and keep moving.* We grabbed hands and pushed with all our might into the storm. It felt like we were pushing giant bales of hay.

As we tired, we wondered if we would ever get home. Then, we recalled what we hadn't done. *Pray.*

We stopped right there. "Heavenly Father, we are lost, please help us get home."

I pulled my scarf over my nose and mouth, but still the sharp snow pushed hard against my numb face and my stiff and freezing fingers. Then suddenly I thought I heard a voice. For a moment, Arnie and I stopped walking on the uneven ground to listen. Hearing nothing, we began walking again. This time my brother heard something, and we stopped to listen.

Again, a voice came faintly. "Arnold, Rose, can you hear me?" Muffled with the whistling of the wind came snatches that scarcely sounded like our names.

Removing the scarves from our mouths, we screamed, "We're here! This is Arnold and Rose. Is that you, Mama?"

We strained our eyes for a glimmer of light through the dense white blinding snow and uncovered our ears listening for the sound of her voice. At last, we spied the faint light of her lantern and struggled through the snow toward it. Finally, we saw her form and fell into her arms.

She said, "Thank you, Lord. Now please help us to go home the rest of the way."

We struggled back to the farm, but it was easier with our mama in the middle. Home at last, she gave us some hot tea and buttered bread. We relaxed around the crackling fire and retold our story.

Taking a bite of Mama's bread with butter and cinnamon sugar on top, I said, "I heard your voice, Mama. And it was right after we prayed!"

Just as my mother heard the faint voice of her mother calling her toward safety, our loving Savior calls us. As the Gospel tells us, "My sheep listen to my voice...I give them eternal life...they shall never perish" (John 10:27–28).

What a gift we have in a relationship with the Savior/Shepherd—Jesus. If we believe in him, we will recognize his voice and follow him. "For it is by believing in your heart that you are made right with God" (Romans 10:10 NLT).

Do you recognize the voice of the Shepherd? Literal sheep will not follow any other voice but that of their shepherd. According to one source online, "In the first century, a single sheep pen held multiple flocks, so it was essential for the sheep to know and recognize their own shepherd's voice....Knowing the Lord's voice indicates experiential knowledge through a relationship with him."[3]

Do we know the Lord's voice well enough to recognize it? Immersing ourselves in God's Word will help us know that voice.

If you haven't ever confessed your sin and agreed with God that you are a sinner, just say this simple prayer: "Thank you God for loving me and sending your Son to die for my sins. I sincerely repent of my sins and receive Christ as my personal Savior. Now as your child, I turn my life over to you."

In the snowstorms of life, where we experience swirling winds and blinding storms, it is good to know the Good Shepherd. He's there, waiting for us to follow him.

How has God lead you out of the storms of your life?
Write about it below:

_____

_____

_____

_____

_____

_____

_____

_____

_____

_____

_____

_____

_____

_____

Tenacious Love

Marriage: Love is the reason.
Lifelong friendship is the gift.
Till death do us part is the length.
—Fawn Weaver[4]

If you've been married to the same person for some time, you may feel you couldn't love anyone as much as you love your spouse. I can understand that, because that's how I felt before my first husband, Bill, died. The man I married was *my* man. I had no doubt when I got married that he was the right one for me.

We were sixteen and nineteen when we met. It didn't take long to know we were meant for each other. Our relationship moved quickly after that first date. Though I was normally shy around boys, I felt totally comfortable with him. We couldn't stop talking. He waited until our third date to kiss me—and I was ready for that kiss. After that evening, I floated into the house with the memory. Soon we were a couple. I couldn't wait to be with Bill every minute of every day.

I still remember those tummy-fluttery times, even more than fifty years later. Before long, we were talking about marriage. We became officially engaged after high school. His graduation gift to me was a diamond ring.

I wish I could say we lived happily ever after, but I cannot. Very quickly, we developed a pattern of arguments, silent treatments, and making up. We argued about the normal things couples struggle with: parenting, finances, and sex. Bill and I became "comfortable" with the norm, even though we weren't happy. We were two stubborn people wanting our own way.

"Look," Bill said one evening after another quarrel. "I can't take this anymore. Do you think a counselor might be able to help us?"

We saw a series of counselors. One helped us identify our dysfunctional marriage as a patient. Bill and I were doctors tasked with diagnosing the problem, determining the cure, and healing the patient/marriage. "How do you want your history to read?" another counselor challenged.

One morning in Sunday School, the teacher gave a routine call for prayer requests. Members usually brought up needs for healing or employment.

To my surprise, Bill raised his hand. "Shirley and I are having difficulties in our marriage and we're going to counseling," he said. "I'd like prayer for us to work out our problems."

I looked down at my lap in embarrassment, pretending to read my notes. Marriage problems were never discussed openly in our group. At the same time, I felt relief. That open, honest request and the willingness to acknowledge that we needed help began to turn things around.

In addition to that prayer request in the Sunday school class, a couples' communication class our counselor recommended bridged the gap between Bill and me. In order to change things, we needed to talk about our problems. This was tough for me, as I would often clam up in fear of angering Bill. In the class, we learned to repeat things back to each other, really listening to what the other was saying instead of just wanting to be heard ourselves.

It seems such a simple thing, yet we had to let go of our stubbornness in thinking the other person needed to change. That key element—listening and repeating back what the other person said—made a major transformation in our marriage.

We began a new intimacy with each other, not just the oneness of sexual intimacy but heart intimacy. We felt freer to share our inner thoughts with each other. I began to trust, revealing my true feelings to Bill. He felt safe revealing himself to me as well. We found ways to be a couple, not just two people bobbing in the surf alongside each other, raising our family.

We learned to communicate.

So there are not two, but one. God has joined the two together,
so no one should separate them.
—Matthew 19:6 NCV

Are you in a relationship that you think could have better communication? Where can you start? For me, it took years of asking God to show me, to change me and be more like him.

I prayed Bible verses. One stood out to me: "We capture every thought and make it give up and obey Christ" (2 Corinthians 10:5 NCV).

Write a prayer below for a relationship you believe could be closer. It could be your spouse or a friend or a family member.

_____

_____

_____

_____

_____

Even When Afraid, I Will Trust

*For God did not give us a Spirit of fear
but of power and love and self-control.*
—2 Timothy 1:7 NET

My first husband, Bill, came through the door with a frown on his face.

"Hi, honey," I said. As I tried to give him a hug, he pushed me away. I immediately returned to my old way of handling his rejection. Phrases ran through my head. *What did I say? Did I do something wrong? Is he mad at me?* I hated conflict and would do anything to avoid it.

For twenty years, Bill and I had struggled. We fought. Argued. Sometimes over the same things. Then we made up. But since we'd learned to communicate, I'd committed to taking a different approach.

The verse that says God did not give us a spirit of fear had a compelling effect on me. I realized I didn't need to be afraid when conflict came. I asked the Holy Spirit to give me the strength not to fear Bill's reactions. That afternoon, instead of giving in to my usual response—thinking I'd done something wrong—I decided to confront his anger, remembering the verse I'd been meditating on.

I walked into our bedroom, "Look, I'm not sure what's going on here, but I'm not going to take on your anger. You might have good reason to be upset, but I know I'm not the cause of it." Then I left the room.

A while later, he stepped into the kitchen. "I'm not mad at you. Something happened at work. I need to go for a hike and work it out."

My challenge to him had helped both of us. Displaying a spirit of courage by speaking up instead of cowering under fear, made a difference then and in the years to come. We enjoyed less conflict and more love and respect. As time passed, we began to trust each other more with our emotions.

> Perhaps your fear isn't conflict in your marriage.
> It might be in the workplace, with your children, or your parents.
> Ask God to show you where you might show courage to state your needs or feelings. Write a prayer below.

_____

_____

_____

_____

_____

_____

_____

_____

Unfamiliar Paths

*I will lead the blind by ways they have not known,
along unfamiliar paths I will guide them.*
—Isaiah 42:16

"Are we on the right trail? I think we've been on this one too long." There were four of us: me, my daughter, and her two sons, ages eight and nine. I had climbed this peak numerous times and so had my daughter.

It was a challenging, nearly sixteen-mile, out-and-back hike with a 4,500-foot gain in altitude called Table Mountain. The views were spectacular with Mount Rainier and Mount Hood right in front of us.

We'd scrambled up the 4,500 feet to the top, walked across the flat, green meadow that was like a table, oohed and aahed at the fabulous view on top, and cautioned the boys not to get too close to the edge of the steep cliff.

Now we were ready to be done.

Hot and sweaty, we climbed over rocks and rubble down the steep path to return to the trailhead. Finally, we were on more level ground and stepped up our pace, sensing we were nearly done.

Soon, the trail did not look familiar any longer. We read in the trail guide, "There are several routes from here, and the trail is a bit of a maze." Yup. We were lost. And tired. Our snacks were eaten and our water bottles nearly empty.

I took out my cell phone, glad to have service, punched in my son's number, and asked for help. He'd climbed it many times and had a great memory of where the maze of trails led down to the parking lot. Finally with his help, we were on the right trail.

God promises us guidance as we traverse this life too. I was encouraged this morning. After writing down some concerns I had, I read, "For I am the Lord your God who takes hold of your right hand and says to you, Do not fear; I will help you" (Isaiah 41:13).

Lord, please forgive me
when I think I won't be able to accomplish something
I believe you have told me to do. You remind us not to fear.
You promise to help us and take hold of our hands
to guide us along unfamiliar paths.
Thank you for the reminder and help me to depend on you always.

Write down some concerns you have. Ask God to guide you. Copy Isaiah 41:13 above to remind yourself you are not alone.

_____

_____

_____

_____

_____

Remembering to Rest

There is a place of quiet rest,
Near to the heart of God,
A place where sin cannot molest,
Near to the heart of God.
—"Quiet Rest" by Cleland McAfee (1866–1944)[5]

A pastor and choir leader wrote the words to "Quiet Rest" after hearing the dreadful news that his two young nieces had died within twenty-four hours of each other from diphtheria. McAfee was so burdened and in such grief for himself and his brother's family that, he wrote this hymn. His congregational choir learned it and sang it in front of the darkened, quarantined house the following Sunday in 1903.

Although retired, both my husband Jim and I have felt extremely busy. It seems we have more on our schedule than ever, including more time at the computer and on our phones. So we decided to take a break from our devices for a twenty-four-hour period. We dubbed it a "tech sabbath." Instead of being glued to a device, Jim and I read, walked outdoors, and talked more. It was peaceful. Restful. We felt more connected with each other.

Whenever I walked by our charging station, I itched to stop and punch the home button on my phone to see what was new. But as the day went on, it wasn't as important to check. Each time I was tempted to check my phone, I prayed, *Thank you, Lord, that you are always present*. I was surprised that I didn't miss my devices as much as I had expected.

The next day, we turned them back on. There were no urgent messages. No compelling emails. The world got along fine with our taking a break.

When the Apostle Paul had the vision of Jesus on the road to Damascus, he believed that Jesus was the Messiah, and he left his life of persecuting the Christians. He became one of them. After his conversion, Paul tells us, "When this happened, I did not rush out to consult with any human being. Nor did I go up to Jerusalem to consult with those who were apostles before I was. Instead, I went away into Arabia, and later I returned to the city of Damascus" (Galatians 1:17–18).

Whether it's dealing with grief, managing your online presence, or making a major life-change, prioritizing time to enter into God's rest is crucial to cultivating hope.

Lord, thank you that you are as near as a thought and always available. Help me as I analyze my time on the devices I use. I would like that quiet rest with you.

Is there a day that you believe you can turn your device off and take a sabbath from it? Write a plan below:

_____

_____

_____

_____

Surprised by Joy

The Lord is my strength and my song;
he has given me victory.
This is my God, and I will praise him.
—Exodus 15:2, NLT

Two years passed after my husband Bill died. I yearned for a soulmate again. A bright light came into my life and changed it forever. The moment Blair and I met, the angst of my loss scuttled away like dried leaves blown about on a windy day.

We met for dinner and found we really enjoyed each other's company. The date lasted until the restaurant closed for the night. Within a month, we were engaged, and we married six months later. Our families blended wonderfully. Our adjustment to marriage was as close as possible to heaven on earth.

During our first summer together, we planned a trip to South Africa, where Blair's late wife had been born and grown up. He wanted me to experience the beautiful country with him.

On that trip, I had to pinch myself to believe the sights on our safari in the vast African bush. "Look over there," I whispered to

Blair from the safety of our land cruiser. We watched a leopard leap up into a large tree, straddle a large limb, and take a nap. There was a pride of lions, rhinoceroses, elephants, and African buffalos, all part of the Big Five.

We drove through 300-year-old vineyards and rented a simply furnished, refurbished Dutch cape house with whitewashed walls and a thatched roof. I talked Blair into climbing the famous Table Mountain in the hot African sun. We jumped the waves in the Indian Ocean, ate superb seafood, and marveled at the converging of two oceans at Cape Point. For six weeks, we enjoyed the summertime climate south of the equator.

We returned home two days before the New Year, basking in the memories of our wonderful trip. "Let's do this again," I said. "You could be the tour guide."

> *In their hearts humans plan their course,*
> *but the LORD establishes their steps.*
> —Proverbs 16:9

Where have you planned a course for your life, but instead God surprised you with a different good thing?
It's good to look back to see how God has worked in your life.
Ask God to help you remember and write it down below.
You might be surprised.

_____

_____

_____

_____

Who Was He?

For he will order his angels to protect you wherever you go.
They will hold you up with their hands
so you won't even hurt your foot on a stone.
—Psalm 91:11–12 NLT

"I don't know if I can make it!" I moaned.

It was a bright, sunny day in February in the White River Canyon on Mt. Hood. Cross-country skiing was a new hobby for my husband Bill and me. We loved the winter wonderland. No ski lifts and lines of people. Just the beauty of the wilderness. The snow-covered trail had a crust of ice, but it hadn't mattered, because we were skiing uphill—easier to navigate for a cross-country skier. However, when we reached the end of the canyon and turned around, we had to descend.

I kept falling as we skied along the downward-sloping, ice-crusted snow. Each time I struggled to get up, my recently injured knee would throb. I'd fallen multiple times now and was getting tired. *Am I going to make it?*

There was no other way but to keep moving down the trail. Soon, a single skier came alongside us. We hadn't noticed him before. We chatted about skiing and how much we enjoyed the outdoors. He casually gave us some techniques that helped us maneuver down the slope, and I became more confident and didn't fall as much. Finally, we reached a flatter portion of the canyon, and the trail was easier to navigate.

And then, just like that, the man was gone. He didn't say good-bye. He wasn't in front of or behind us. There was nowhere to go but back to the highway. Where was he?

On our way home, we discussed the solo skier. "That was weird. He just appeared out of nowhere," my husband said. "I didn't see him on the trail up the canyon, did you?"

I shook my head. "All of a sudden, he wasn't with us. He just disappeared. Could he have been an angel?"

We believed he was. God's Word says, "He will order his angels to protect you" (Psalm 91:11 NLT). Even better, God gave his only Son to offer us eternal life. "For this is how God loved the world: He gave his one and only Son, so that everyone who believes in him will not perish but have eternal life. God sent his Son into the world not to judge the world, but to save the world through him" (John 3:16-17 NLT).

Lord, thank you for loving us so much you sent your only Son to rescue us.
Now we can know you when we believe in Jesus Christ.
Help me remember the beautiful gift you've given.
Eternal life. And sometimes, you send an angel to help us.
In Jesus's name, amen.

Angels are created beings, just as we are; they should never be worshipped. And I believe God brought the angel—the lone skier—to help us in a precarious situation. Sometimes we might not even be aware they've helped us. We don't worship the angels, but we do thank God for how they are used to impact our lives.

Write a prayer of thanks to God on the next page.

What is it to Ponder?

*But Mary treasured up all these things
and pondered them in her heart.*
—Luke 2:20

"Don't push!" the nurse told me. I ignored her and kept pushing. I didn't care if the doctor wasn't there. I did what my body told me to do. Push. Push hard. And moments later, she was born. There were complications in that delivery, but all the painful moments were forgotten after the nurse announced, "It's a girl!"

Mothers who give birth have really gone from death to life. In a few short moments, they've lost pounds from the baby's weight and all the fluids along with the baby. It is a shock to a woman's system. She is giddy. Relieved.

After taking care of my baby—she had some breathing problems—the hospital staff took care of me. They covered me with warm blankets as my teeth chattered from giving birth. And I pondered. *Ponder* means to consider something deeply and thoroughly.

I pondered while the doctors tried to figure out why our daughter was very ill. They performed multiple tests and discovered she'd lost seventy-five percent of her blood during labor. Quickly, they gave her a blood transfusion, and several hours later, she was fine. They called her a miracle baby.

Mary, the mother of God, pondered after giving birth to Jesus. She must have experienced what we mothers do after giving birth: exhilaration, giddiness, relief. Mary named him Jesus because the angel told her she would give birth to the Son of God and to name him Jesus. Don't you think she pondered that fact after she touched her baby's creamy cheek? Kissed his sweet head? Examined his fingers and toes? She pondered this miracle baby she gave birth to. "But Mary treasured up all these things and pondered them in her heart" (Luke 2:19).

Thank you, heavenly Father, for sending your Son to be with us, Emmanuel—God with us. Amen.

How often do we take for granted the process of giving birth? What would it be like to give birth to God? He became flesh and became one of us. Ponder with me that fact. God in flesh. Let it sink in.

Write a prayer of thanks to God the Father,
who sent his only Son to earth.

_____

_____

_____

_____

_____

_____

How About a Spiritual Diet?

*No discipline is enjoyable while it is happening—it's painful!
But afterward there will be a peaceful harvest of right living
for those who are trained in this way.*
—Hebrews 12:11 NLT

"Oof!" I exclaimed as I tugged at the zipper of my favorite pair of slacks. I'd been steadily gaining a few pounds. A tasty dessert here, a piece of pastry with my coffee there. Now, I could barely snap the hook and had to ask my husband to help me zip the pants while I grasped both sides of the fabric, holding my stomach in while he zipped it to the top. *Something has got to give.*

That began the eating program I am on and have been for some months. This isn't a quick plan to drop some pounds and then return to my old way of eating. No, I've found I need to change some of my eating patterns permanently. My hope is that when I go to my yearly physical, I'll be told my cholesterol numbers are improving, my weight is better, my overall health is excellent, and I'm fit for my age.

"Are you not aware that you are the temple of God, and that the Spirit of God dwells in you? If anyone defiles the temple of God, God will destroy him. For the temple of God is holy, which temple you are" (1 Corinthians 3:16–17 NMB). What an honor it is to think our bodies are temples where the Spirit dwells!

How about a spiritual "eating program"? We want our minds to be absorbing healthy thoughts and words so we can make better decisions. We test what God's will might be in our life through the renewing of our minds. "Do not conform to the pattern of this world, but be transformed by the renewing of your mind. Then you will be able to test and approve what God's will is—his good, pleasing and perfect will" (Romans 12:2).

While good eating habits are important, more so is renewing our minds. If we desire to know God's will, we must immerse ourselves in his Word. We "eat" the right words that show us who God is and how much he loves us and what his will for us is.

Remember, "No discipline is enjoyable while it is happening—it's painful! But afterward there will be a peaceful harvest of right living for those who are trained in this way" (Hebrews 12:11).

Lord, I want to know your good and perfect will.
I realize I need to read your Word in order to know what that is.
Help me as I read your Word.
Renew my mind so I can know your will for me. Thank you, amen.

I'm looking forward to the peaceful harvest of better numbers medically, yes, but more than that, the harvest of a transformed mind through spiritual discipline.

How about you? Is it time for a spiritual diet? Make a plan to start—or end—your day with time in God's Word. Find a Bible study at your church.

Write a prayer on the next page
asking God to find a way to make that happen.

A New Heart

I will give you a new heart and put a new spirit in you; I will remove from you your heart of stone and give you a heart of flesh.
—Ezekiel 36:26

Oh Lord, I prayed. Are you going to heal Bill? He isn't getting any better. You know I've been praying his heart would be changed. Would you please heal him? I begged.

For years, I had prayed that my husband's complacent heart would be compliant towards God. Did he get this illness to turn towards God? To make his stony heart one of flesh?

When he found out he had chronic leukemia, he told me, "I don't have much time, so I'm going to do everything I can while I am still physically able." That meant climbing expeditions, rock climbing, and later, training his dog for hunt tests. Even though Bill believed in God and had accepted Jesus as his Savior, his activities came before anything, including family events or church.

I kept praying for his stony heart. Gradually, I began to see changes. Before leaving for work in the mornings, I noticed he was reading his Bible.

And then, disaster struck. He became very ill with a virus—the shingles virus. It didn't go away. Weeks and weeks of debilitating pain. He couldn't work. He had to confine himself in our darkened bedroom because the light hurt his eyes so much.

One morning during my morning prayer and Bible reading, I came across a verse. "Is anyone among you sick? Let them call the elders of the church to pray over them and anoint them with oil in the name of the Lord" (James 5:14–16). I asked Bill if I should call our pastor and the elders of our church to come and pray for him. Instead of the no I expected from him, he said, "Call them."

An hour later, they came. We sat on the sofa, Bill in his pajamas, a blanket over his legs. I sat beside him. He confessed some things he believed were wrong in his life—common, ordinary things that we all struggle with. One elder dabbed oil on him. We prayed for healing from shingles and also for forgiveness.

"I want what she has," he said, pointing to me. *Me?* For so long, I had been praying that my beloved would know the length and breadth of God's love, as I was beginning to know it. And yet, in bursts of anger, he would often accuse me of being a terrible Christian. I bowed my head, amazed and grateful for his words.

I expected complete physical healing. Instead, his heart was dramatically changed. His attitude was different. He was grateful for everything I did to help him feel better. The swearing stopped. He asked me to read his Bible and other devotional books out loud to him because the virus prevented his eyes from focusing on any screen or book.

He often asked me to pray with him—not about healing but for others.

My husband was healed. Not physically, but spiritually. His heart had become a heart of flesh.

Lord, we all have stony hearts at times.

*Give me faith to believe you will answer my prayers.
If it is my heart that is hard toward you,
please make my heart a heart of flesh. In Jesus's name, amen.*

Do you have someone in your life who has a stony heart? It could be your husband, a child, or a sibling. Pray for their stony heart and ask God to give them a heart of flesh. "I will give you a new heart and put a new spirit in you; I will remove from you your heart of stone and give you a heart of flesh" (Ezekiel 36:26).

Write your thoughts or prayer below.

_____
_____
_____
_____
_____
_____
_____
_____
_____
_____
_____
_____

The Tale of a Baseball Mitt

*So now there is no condemnation for those who belong to Christ Jesus.
And because you belong to him, the power of the life-giving Spirit
has freed you from the power of sin that leads to death.*
—Romans 1:1-2 NLT

It was the spring of 1960. Ten-year-old Jimmy had saved his paper-route money to buy a coveted baseball mitt he'd been eyeing for weeks. Nearly every day, he rode his bike to Lloyd Center, the shopping center near his home, and looked at the mitts on display at his favorite shop, Toyland. Finally, he had $5—enough to buy that left-handed mitt for first base, the usual position he played in Little League.

There it was! It fit his hand perfectly, as if it were made just for him. And then he turned over the glove to check the price: $5.99. He'd saved his money for weeks and only had $5. What to do? He looked at some of the other mitts, but he really wanted this one. Then he spied a mitt with the price tag of $4.99. They didn't have bar codes in those days, just a sticky white square displaying the price. No one was around, so Jimmy quickly switched the tags.

"Four ninety-nine!" the salesclerk said.

Jimmy handed over his dollar bills.

"Here you go." The clerk placed the mitt in a bag and gave him the penny change.

Jimmy carefully placed the mitt on the back of his bicycle and rode home. But instead of being excited about the purchase, he began to feel very guilty. Each time he used the mitt at practice, it worked really well, but there was always this cloud of guilt surrounding it. He wished he'd never swapped the tags.

Years passed and Jimmy—now my husband Jim—never forgot that act. As a young adult he told himself he'd just go back to the store and give them the extra dollar he owed, but the store was no longer there. Eventually, Jim professed his faith in Jesus Christ. He invited him to enter his life and make him a new person. Christ did just that. He entered his life, forgave his sins, and gave him eternal life with him.

Since that time, Jim still slips and makes errors in word or deed—sins—but he has been forgiven! "For everyone has sinned; we all fall short of God's glorious standard. Yet God, in his grace, freely makes us right in his sight. He did this through Christ Jesus when he freed us from the penalty for our sins" (Romans 3:23–24). Jim has Christ living in him and that helps him do what's right.

He often reads through the longest chapter of the Bible, Psalm 119. It is a psalm focusing on the Word of God and how it helps us live. "I have hidden your word in my heart that I might not sin against you" (Psalm 119:11). "Teach me, Lord, the way of your decrees, that I may follow it to the end" (Psalm 119:33). "Your word is a lamp for my feet, a light on my path" (Psalm 119:105).

The Word of God is available to you as well as to Jim and me. Seek it. Read it. It will give hope and reason to trust the God of Abraham, Isaac, and you and me!

Today, take the time to read Psalm 119—all the way to the end.

Reflect on it and write down some things you learned from it.

This Old House

*"Do not let your hearts be troubled. You believe in God;
believe also in me. My Father's house has many rooms;
if that were not so, would I have told you that I am going there
to prepare a place for you? And if I go and prepare a place for you,
I will come back and take you to be with me that you also may be
where I am. You know the way to the place where I am going."*
—John 14:1–4

The house stood cold and empty. I walked in the front door where there was once a large room with the dining area on one end and the living room on the other. Now there was an ugly wall dividing the area. It didn't look anything like the home I remembered growing up in. The opening of a once-red-brick fireplace was blocked off. They'd painted the red bricks white. The lovely dining room with a large, arched mirror and built-in China closet was gone. I walked past what once held a built-in dinette with bright-red, leather-like upholstery. Gone. Many nights I'd sat there, doing my homework.

The kitchen looked mostly the same. So did the bedrooms. Empty of course.

When I had grown up there, it was a parsonage. I moved into the house with my family at age twelve. I left the house at age nineteen as a young bride. Years later, each time my husband and I would drive past that house where so many changes in my life happened, I'd point out the three windows on the upstairs level. "There's my old room," I'd say. In that room, I dreamed. I planned. I cried. I prayed. I wish I could show you a photo of what it once looked like, so bright in my memory. But I cannot.

Now the church is tearing down the old house to make room for additional buildings. When I heard that would happen, I asked to tour the home one last time before it was gone. This cold, empty house was so unlike the house I'd lived in. Then it was always active, with people coming and going. Good smells like bread baking. The aroma of pork roast in the oven. Each Christmas, Mom would invite all the people in the church to come to the house for an open house. She'd baked dozens of cookies. Of course, we helped her, but she was the force behind the entertainment. This was a busy house.

After the tour, I felt satisfied. It wasn't what it once was anyway. The memories of life in that house were more important than the building itself. And they're still there, clear in my mind. The voices. The smells.

One day, I'll be gone, and those memories gone with me. But it's all right. I know my heavenly home will have a new interior. "My Father's house has many rooms; if that were not so, would I have told you that I am going there to prepare a place for you?" (John 14:2). It will be new and special.

Each day grows closer to the time when I will leave this earth. My body will go to a plot that's already been purchased in the cemetery near that house that will no longer stand. But my spirit will go to my new home where I will live eternally. It will be more beautiful than anyone can imagine.

Dear Lord Jesus, I ask you to be with each person reading this devotional and help them to think back to their childhood. Help them resolve the good or bad, letting go of what was not good and enjoying the pleasant memories. In your name Jesus, amen.

What are your memories of a home you grew up in?
Write down one of them, pleasant or not.
Ask God to help you forgive and heal from any wounds that took place there and to remember and relish the good that happened.

_____

_____

_____

_____

_____

_____

_____

_____

_____

_____

_____

_____

_____

Part II

Anchored in *Encouragement*

Safety Under the Feathers

Those who live in the shelter of the Most High
will find rest in the shadow of the Almighty.
This I declare about the Lord: He alone is my refuge, my place of safety;
he is my God, and I trust him. He will cover you with his feathers.
He will shelter you with his wings.
His faithful promises are your armor and protection.
—Psalms 91:1–2 NLT

A devastating forest fire destroyed acres and acres of beautiful forest land. After the fire had been contained, one of the firefighters noticed a carcass of a large bird along the trail. *Why didn't the bird fly away instead of staying on the forest floor?* he wondered. As he drew closer, he nudged the body to the side and was startled by four small birds who came from underneath their mother's body and ran/flew down the trail. Alive! The mother bird had protected her babies by covering them with her feathers.

Just as those baby chicks were protected by their mama, we can be protected by God's shelter.

My husband Jim and I have been meeting with a trainer to keep our bodies as strong as is possible. Just as we need to work our muscles to remain strong and do things to keep our balance as we age, we also need to work our spiritual muscles by reading the promises God provides us in his Word. There is truth and strength there, so when the fires come, we know where to run for safety. "His faithful promises are *our* armor and protection" (Psalm 91:2 NLT).

Looking back over my life, I've learned in the difficult moments and scary times that if I went to God for refuge and safety—just like the chicks under their mama's body were sheltered—I felt the safety of his protection. There were still troubles, but when I ran to him, I felt secure. I knew I wasn't alone.

Once, in deep despair while at my husband Bill's bedside, I heard singing down the hall in the hospital. The deep alto voice sang familiar gospel songs, and my spirit was encouraged. Another time, I felt there was nowhere to turn, and an old family friend just showed up to be with me. Another time, a friend brought some nourishing food while I waited in the hospital for news and didn't want to leave Bill's bedside.

Perhaps you are at a good time in your life. It might be someone else that needs a boost. A hug. An encouraging note. A tasty meal. Sitting alongside a friend, you don't always have to say something, just be there with them. Write out the verse about God's protection on an index card and share it. Keep it handy for yourself. It's always a good reminder.

> What can you do to give encouragement to someone?
> List some people who might need it.
> Don't forget to write out the verse from Psalm 91:1–2.
> Keep it handy to give to someone or to encourage yourself.

Name: _____

How I Can Encourage: _____

Name: _____

How I Can Encourage: _____

_____

_____

Name: _____

How I Can Encourage: _____

_____

_____

_____

_____

_____

_____

_____

_____

_____

_____

We Learn to Become One

*But in fact God has placed the parts in the body,
every one of them, just as he wanted them to be.*
—1 Corinthians 12:18

After twenty years of stubbornness on both Bill's and my part, our marriage was transformed from two separate people navigating through life to a oneness we hadn't experienced until that vulnerable prayer request and the couples' communication class. We could have limped along for twenty more years, and our final good-bye would have been different. Instead, Bill and I learned how to communicate, merging into one through our conversations.

Two words we learned to avoid were *always* and *never*. We began using the phrase, *I feel* to replace *you made me feel*. We took ownership of our feelings. We also learned that some things weren't worth arguing about.

For years, Bill had done his thing and I had done mine. Now we purposed to do things together.

"I've always wanted to climb Mt. Hood. Would you be willing to do it with me?" Bill asked one evening.

I enjoyed keeping my body in shape and hiking outdoors sounded like a good thing to me. So I agreed to take the mountaineering class.

We enjoyed each step of the journey as we trained, shopped for gear, and accomplished the graduation climb. It was something I'd never dreamed of doing, and I *enjoyed* it! I pushed back my fear of heights to ascend steep-edged trails.

After our graduation climb, we backpacked, rock-climbed, and continued mountaineering. Our kids joined us for some adventures, but many we did alone. Our relationship gradually was transformed.

Over the next twenty years, we never went back to our old ways of handling our disagreements. We learned how to respect each other. And it gave me courage to do things I was scared to do. Our marriage helped both of us to depend on God through the tough times and enjoy the happy times.

After Bill became ill from the shingles virus, the last six months of our forty-and-one-half years together weren't easy. He was hospitalized numerous times. Five months after our pastor and elders prayed over him, Bill suffered with post-herpetic neuralgia and depression from the extreme pain.

In the sixth month, he began to feel better. But then he suffered a small stroke and subsequently suffered a fatal stroke. My children and I were with him that early morning when he drew his last breath.

I was brokenhearted when Bill died, but the changes that had taken place in our marriage also left me with a deep sense of gratitude. And gratitude is more powerful than grief.

Lord, I am grateful for how our marriage
was transformed into a beautiful thing.
It was you who helped us find a common ground
to help our marriage become one,
just as you wanted us to be (1 Corinthians 12:18). Thank You.
In Jesus's name, amen.

What are the unique qualities in you and in those closest to you?
Write a prayer below, thanking God for the way
he designed each of you.

_____

_____

_____

_____

_____

_____

_____

_____

_____

_____

_____

_____

Commit to seeking common ground with your spouse, a good friend, a person you work with, or someone in your church body by carefully listening to the things they say to you.

Entertaining Angels

*For he guards the course of the just
and protects the way of his faithful ones.*
—Proverbs 2:8

Ahead of me, Bill's truck swerved again.

"Oh God, help him!" I screamed, watching helplessly from behind in my own car. We had just passed through a busy intersection with eight lanes of traffic. Bill was an experienced pilot, a confident boat captain, he raced sports cars. Now he was driving as though someone possessed him.

The previous evening, my husband had suffered a TIA (a small stroke), and after a long wait in the ER, they sent us home. The next day, we were to meet for lunch. It was there at that busy intersection of four lanes each way where I'd witnessed the scary event.

A day later, while in my husband's hospital room, I was in anguish. He had been hospitalized many times since he'd been ill from the complications of chronic leukemia, and I was desperately trying to be strong for him. But all I wanted to do was collapse in a puddle of tears.

A student nurse was caring for the patient in the other bed. She noticed my agony. "Come here," she said. With her large, soft body, she took me in her arms and held me tightly. She didn't say a word, just held me. It felt like a hug from God.

Later I thought more about that warm hug. It was a Sunday. Student nurses don't work on Sundays. I believe that fluffy teddy bear of a woman was an angel.

We never know when we encounter angels, but we are reminded in Hebrews 13:2, "Do not forget to show hospitality to strangers, for by so doing some people have shown hospitality to angels without knowing it."

Lord, as I look back on my life, I realize you were with me time after time.
You sent human beings to help me through those tough times.
And possibly, some of them were angels. Thank you. Amen.

Have you experienced something you couldn't explain as a natural occurrence? Could it be you encountered an angel?
If you have, describe it below.

_____

_____

_____

_____

_____

_____

_____

Renewed Strength

But those who hope in the L̲o̲r̲d̲ will renew their strength.
They will soar on wings like eagles;
they will run and not grow weary,
they will walk and not be faint.
—Isaiah 40:31

"Isn't that an eagle?" I exclaimed, looking up at the sky in front of my house.

My neighbor paused her walk by my home. "I've noticed him circling around your house all day."

The presence of the eagle in my neighborhood was reassuring to me. Just one week earlier, my husband Bill had died. I had been living with someone my entire adult life, and now I was alone. At his memorial service, we'd chosen to read the above passage about eagles.

When I saw that eagle, slowly circling the air above, it was as though Bill were watching over me. It wasn't him, but it was a symbol of God's watchful care over me.

I found comfort during those lonely days through my Bible reading and also through little examples of God's presence. "The L̲o̲r̲d̲ watches over the alien and sustains the fatherless and the widow" (Psalm 147:9). "For your Maker is your husband—the LORD Almighty is his name—the Holy One of Israel is your Redeemer" (Isaiah 54:5).

The sight of an eagle gave a glimpse of God's presence to encourage and strengthen me. God will sustain us in difficult times. Like the eagle soaring over my house when I'd never seen an eagle there before. A reminder I wasn't alone.

Father, thank you for your presence in our lives
even through your creatures. The sight of that eagle gave me hope
and caused me to look to you for all my needs.
Thank you for loving me so much. In your Son's name, Jesus, amen.

Can you encourage someone who needs a dose of cheer? I've found writing a short note or text or making a phone call helps them know they aren't alone and blesses me that I've encouraged someone else.

Think of someone who needs a friendly voice today, then find a colorful greeting card and write them a note.

Below, write a prayer for that person.

_____

_____

_____

_____

_____

_____

_____

The Scent of the Master

*Thanks be to God who leads us, wherever we are,
on his own triumphant way and makes our knowledge of him spread
throughout the world like a lovely perfume!
We Christians have the unmistakeable "scent" of Christ,
discernible alike to those who are being saved
and to those who are heading for death.
To the latter it seems like the very smell of doom,
to the former it has the fresh fragrance of life itself.*
—2 Corinthians 2: 14–16 PHILLIPS

My husband Bill's black Labrador retriever, Card, barked and yipped as my son and I passed his run on our walk back from the store. Why was Card so excited and happy when we were so sad? Two days earlier, Bill had died. We'd believed he would tough it out after a major stroke, but we were wrong. The whole family grieved, including Card.

He was an extraordinary hunting dog. Friends jokingly called him Bullet because he was so fast at retrieving ducks and geese. Always by his master's side, he loved working in the field with Bill.

When Todd and I walked to the store to get some fresh air, Todd had grabbed the nearest jacket in the closet—Bill's olive-green hunting jacket. As we walked back home, Card began yipping passionately. He was normally a very quiet dog, and I never heard him bark. Why was Card making all that noise? Then it dawned on me. My son was wearing Bill's jacket. Card *smelled* his master! He sensed his master was home at last.

As Christians, sometimes we can be unaware of our influence on other people. Our attitude and closeness with Christ living in us gives us his fragrance—a "lovely perfume." As a reminder, the Apostle Paul continues in the next chapter of 2 Corinthians, "We dare to say such things because of the confidence we have in God through Christ, and not because we are confident of our own powers" (2 Corinthians 3:4–5 PHILLIPS).

Card didn't understand where his master was, but when he smelled that jacket, he was sure his master was near.

Lord, help your fragrance in me draw others to yourself.
It is not me who does it but you in me. Thank you in Jesus's name, amen.

Do we as Christians sometimes forget our influence on other people? Our attitude with Christ in us gives us a fragrance that draws others to Christ. Our ability is not from ourselves, but completely from God.

How can we be more Christlike?
Read Romans 12:1–2. List some ideas below.

_____

_____

_____

_____

Broken Hearts to Mend

࿇

*He comes the broken heart to bind,
the bleeding soul to cure,
and with the treasures of his grace
to enrich the humble poor.*
—From "Hark, the Glad Sound! The Saviour Comes"
by Philip Doddridge, 1702–1751[6]

࿇

My husband Jim and I work with those grieving the death of a loved one, and every week we are reminded of the extreme sadness that envelops them. In the early days of grief, holidays are like salt in a wound. Music that sounds out of tune.

One widow of less than two years said, "This is kind of a hard time. Traditions don't work so well when you're the only one." They'd been married for fifty years.

The presence of my Savior helped me when I was in the depth of grief. He was my constant companion during those lonely days of eating dinner by myself. Going to bed by myself. Getting up in the morning by myself. Or celebrating a holiday without my loved one. The English poet, Philip Doddridge, said it well with the words, "He comes the broken heart to bind, the bleeding soul to cure, and with the treasures of his grace to enrich the humble poor."

A class called GriefShare also helped me recover. The group provided a community where we shared similar emotions, and we learned much from the grief counselors featured in the videos we watched. It included an encouraging book with guided questions and Bible verses that were helpful. You can find a group near you through www.griefshare.org.

Psalm 147:3 NCV says, "He heals the brokenhearted and bandages their wounds." As a child, when I skinned my knee, my mother would put salve on the broken skin and place a bandage on it. It made it hurt much less. God does that for us. He bandages our wounds. He heals our broken hearts, one stitch at a time.

Whether you have a broken heart that needs God's stitching or your soul needs curing, as the song says, "Give it to the healer of broken hearts, Jesus."[7]

Father, for all of us who have broken hearts, please mend them.
You promise to do that, and we ask for your help as we wait. Amen.

Write a prayer below. Ask God to heal your broken heart.

_____

_____

_____

_____

_____

_____

Nothing Can Separate

*For I am convinced that neither death nor life,
neither angels nor demons, neither the present nor the future,
nor any powers, neither height nor depth,
nor anything else in all creation, will be able to separate us
from the love of God that is in Christ Jesus our Lord.*
—Romans 8:38–39

"I'm sorry to tell you your baby is dead," the obstetrician told me. I could scarcely take it in. My baby? The baby who regularly hiccuped? The little one I'd hoped was a girl? The doctor's voice droned on, "We'll send you home, and you can wait until labor begins. The baby is toxic to you, and your body will naturally begin labor."

On the way home, I looked out at the sunny day with eyes that didn't see. In shock, I stared down at my expanding tummy. This was our bonus baby. My tears flowed nonstop.

Three years earlier I had begun to study and read the Bible. Even though I had believed in God for as long as I can remember, Jesus became more real to me as I studied the Bible with other women in my neighborhood. The Bible opened up in fresh, new ways. I became more patient as a mother and more loving as a wife.

Just before I found out my unborn baby had died, we had been studying prayer. As I contemplated the doctor's news, a passage came to my mind. "Pray continually, give thanks in all circumstances; for this is God's will for you in Christ Jesus" (1 Thessalonians 5:17–18). I didn't understand. *How can I give thanks to God for this?* With tears streaming down my face, I prayed, *Lord, I don't feel thankful, but I want to thank you in all circumstances, so I ask you to help me give thanks.* I sensed his peace. I rested in his love for me.

Five days later, they admitted me to the hospital and induced labor, and after two days of labor, they performed a C-section. Moving me to my room on a gurney, the nurse gave me a sympathy card. In it, she quoted Romans 8:38–39 and told me she was praying for me. Her words helped me turn to the One who was with me in this pain.

The first Sunday I attended church after the birth, the pastor spoke on that very passage. "I am convinced that neither death nor life…nor anything else in all creation, will be able to separate us from the love of God that is in Christ Jesus our Lord" (Romans 8:28–39). Once again, I felt that peace. God loved me. He cared about the pain of my loss. And in my pain, there was the assurance I was never far from Christ's love.

Thank you, Lord, that although I never got to meet my baby Carrie here on earth, I know I will meet her in heaven.
Please give comfort to us who need your care.
Thank you that we are never separated from your love. Amen.

Are you mourning a death—or deaths—of a loved one? Perhaps it isn't death, but a marriage that is collapsing. An illness that cannot be cured. Loss of livelihood. Foreclosure on your home. Remember, *nothing* can separate you from the love of God that is in Christ Jesus.

Think about the passage quoted earlier,
"Pray continually, give thanks in all circumstances;

for this is God's will for you in Christ Jesus," (1 Thessalonians 5:17–18). Write a prayer below:

_____

_____

_____

_____

_____

_____

_____

_____

_____

_____

_____

_____

_____

_____

_____

_____

_____

Facing Absence

The presence of absence is everywhere.
—Edna St Vincent Millay[8]

The room might be filled with people. But that one person—the one who is no longer on this earth—makes the room yawn with emptiness. In my years of helping others work through their grief, they often talk about how much they miss their loved one.

During grief, we encourage the grievers to immerse themselves in God's Word. The words of God are healing—passages and promises right there in the Bible.

The passage in Romans 8 continued to sooth my aching mama's heart when I mourned the loss of my stillborn baby. "For I am convinced that neither death nor life, neither angels nor demons, neither the present nor the future, nor any powers, neither height nor depth, nor anything else in all creation, will be able to separate us from the love of God that is in Christ Jesus our Lord" (Romans 8:38–39). Jesus was with me in my anguish as I faced the empty nursery.

During the early days of loss, I read the book of Psalms. The words comforted me. They mirrored my own feelings. I sensed God's presence in the quiet house and the absence of my baby. I could talk to him day or night when others weren't available. He understood like no other. I clung to the words, "He heals the brokenhearted" (Psalms 147:3); "The Lord is close to the brokenhearted" (Psalms 34:8).

Do you have a broken heart? Are you grieving a loss you think you won't get past? Do you feel so alone you can hardly bear it? There is One who understands you. Immerse yourself in God's Word. Let the words soothe your despairing soul. Remember the promise: *Nothing will be able to separate us from the love of God that is in Christ Jesus.*

Lord, please fill the reader with your presence
as they face the presence of absence. Be their comfort.
Be their strength as they face life without the life they loved so much.
You promise to heal the brokenhearted,
and I ask you to do that for this dear soul who grieves so much.

When my heart was hurting, writing in a journal really helped. Keep a notebook just for this purpose. Date each entry in case you decide to go back over your words. I found it encouraging to watch my emotions improve as the weeks went by.

For I am convinced that neither death nor life, neither angels nor demons,
neither the present nor the future, nor any powers,
neither height nor depth, nor anything else in all creation,
will be able to separate us from the love of God
that is in Christ Jesus our Lord.
—Romans 8:38–39

Write out Romans 8:38–39 below.

_____

_____

_____

We Have Hope

*All the days planned for me were written in your book
before I was one day old.*
—Psalm 139:16 NCV

"Shirley, sit down," Mom said one cold, wintry evening. I was returning from an evening shift. She turned up the television volume, and I heard a voice on the ten o'clock news. "Karen Rose Schlecht died from sustaining head injuries." The reporter droned on, but I'd stopped listening. My best friend, gone? Stunned, I could scarcely take it in. I sobbed in my mother's arms.

A bright-eyed girl, Karen lived just down the road from my house. She was a smart, straight-A student. We read together, studied together, and had sleepovers where we shared our deepest secrets. After graduating from high school, our friendship continued.

We often talked about our shared belief in Jesus. At eighteen years old, we were invincible, with our lives in front of us....Now she was gone. It was so hard to believe she was really dead. When I saw her shattered body in the coffin a few days later, I knew it was so.

Although death comes to all, if you believe in Jesus, you will have eternal life. "But to all who believed him and accepted him, he gave the right to become children of God" (John 1:12 NLT). Death is not the end, but the beginning of eternal life. For those who believe in Jesus, we are promised eternal life. That can be a comfort to us when we grieve the loss of someone.

That morning, Karen had gone shopping, and instead of reaching home, she walked into heaven.

Even in my grief, I was comforted that I would see Karen once again. "Brothers and sisters, we want you to know about those Christians who have died so you will not be sad, as others who have no hope" (1 Thessalonians 4:13 NCV).

> *Lord, teach us to number our days. If we are grieving,*
> *thank you for the hope we have of eternal life with you. Amen.*

If you don't have this hope of life beyond death, place your trust in Jesus and repent of your sins. You can start a personal relationship with Jesus right now. Pray this simple prayer:

> *Lord, I understand all of us in the human race are sinners,*
> *and that means me. I believe God took on flesh*
> *and became a human being as Jesus Christ,*
> *that Jesus died on the cross in my place,*
> *and that he rose from the dead to prove he was God.*
> *I know I'm a sinner and ask for forgiveness.*
> *I trust in you, Jesus, to be my Lord and Savior.*
> *Thank you for saving me. Amen.*

If you prayed and believed that prayer, you now belong to Jesus Christ. You are promised eternal life with him in heaven. I'd love it if you would write to me, and I will pray for you. Email me at shirley@shirleymozena.com.

The Dance of a Lifetime

Day by day and with each passing moment,
Strength I find to meet my trials here;
Trusting in my Father's wise bestowment,
I've no cause for worry or for fear.
—Carolina Sandell[9]

One month after the memorable trip Blair and I took to Africa, tragedy struck. Blair felt faint one evening and complained of a headache. As we waited for the ambulance, I knelt by his side, told him I loved him and prayed for the paramedics to help him. I recited Psalm 23, "The Lord is my shepherd, I shall not want. . . ."

Moments later, Blair lost consciousness. The ambulance rushed him to the hospital, and after they diagnosed a brain aneurysm, he died one day later.

It was impossible not question God in my grief as I faced widowhood for a second time. I paced my house, wept gallons of tears. Once more, and in spite of my reluctance to compare my last grief, I knew this would be a long road.

I read books and listened to music. Reading the Bible gave me the most solace. I reviewed our photos from our recent trip, asked for God's comfort on sleepless nights. Again, I dined alone, traveled alone, sat in church by myself. I learned once again that God is fully trustworthy even in my grief.

Ultimately, I chose to be grateful for what Blair and I had. Instead of becoming bitter, I depended on my heavenly Father to take care of me and use me right where I was. The two years of receiving Blair's love had made my life richer and had been worth the risk of marrying again.

A friend wrote this story after she heard about my husband's sudden death.

> This is the story of Shirley. One day, she met Bill when both were very young. They began to dance. It was sometimes awkward. No matter how they tried, they kept stepping on each other's toes. Yet they knew if they looked to the One who created the dance, He would help them, and He did. As the years passed, their dance flowed, smooth and beautiful.
>
> And then, Bill was gone.
>
> Shirley thought she would never dance again. A part of her longed to, but it had taken so much work for her and Bill to get it right, she wasn't sure she had the energy.
>
> Then one day, Shirley met Blair and they began to dance. Their dance was a little faster, but smooth from the start. Both could hardly believe how easy it was, with never an awkward moment. Then, just as quickly as Blair showed up, he was gone. If Shirley had known that her heart would hurt so much, she might not have let Blair have her dance card. But she would have missed the dance of a lifetime.
>
> (Heidi Timm Heaps, 2010)

Have you found yourself in a place you didn't want to be? What did you do? What helped you get through previous griefs—whether it was loss of a loved one or a relationship that was strained or even no longer exists?

Write a letter to God,
asking him to help you as you reflect upon your losses,
and if you haven't yet grieved those losses, ask for his help.

Table for One

The Lord will work out his plans for my life—for your faithful love, O Lord, endures forever. Don't abandon me, for you made me.
—Psalm 138:8 NLT

"For one?" The hostess asked me.

If you go to a restaurant and ask for seating for one, do you get a strange look? How about a seat at a movie or a performance? Whether you are alone because of life's circumstances or have always lived alone and dined by yourself, strange looks might be the response you get. But singleness is becoming more common. Statistics say there are more people renting apartments for one than ever before.

This year, some will celebrate a holiday alone for the first time. Just this week I heard someone say, "I'd just like to go to bed the day before Thanksgiving and wake up January 2!"

Perhaps you don't necessarily *want* to be alone on a given holiday; it just works out that family lives far away, and your spouse is no longer here. Does this sound like you?

Perhaps you don't live alone, but you feel alone. You rarely have conversations with a spouse or roommate except to discuss what might be on the calendar for the day or week.

Widowed twice, I know what it's like to be alone. Sometimes I'd take myself out for dinner and choose a table in a corner where I could observe other diners. In my solitude, I'd imagine what their story might be. There were plenty of couples who sat together, but they would be busy texting and looking at their phones, talking to *other* people who were not even there. They were alone, too.

We are reminded in Psalm 138:8 that God was David's maker and therefore would never abandon him. God won't abandon us either. If you are alone, I suggest you take the plunge and go someplace—a movie, a restaurant, a concert—by yourself. You might be surprised how much you enjoy it. You may even make a friend.

And I am with you always, even to the end of the age.
—Matthew 28:20 NLT

If you attend church, you might ask your pastor if there's a new widow or widower who could use a friend to share a meal with. If you have family around, be aware of anyone who lives alone and invite them to your upcoming holiday meal—Thanksgiving, Christmas, or any other special occasion. Write out a plan below.

_____

_____

_____

_____

_____

A Cheerful Robin

Sometimes we can't see the end of a difficult time.
—Shirley Mozena[10]

Tap, tap, tap. *What was that?* I was sitting in a wicker chair and reading my Bible in the morning room. *Was it a branch hitting the side of the house?* The sound came again. Sighing, I got up and checked the front of the house. Nothing. I heard the persistent tapping again. I checked the garage. Nothing. On my way back, I glanced at the window and noticed a large, red-breasted robin perched on a small tree just outside the window.

Next morning, right on cue, I heard the tapping again. I looked out the window, and there was Mr. Robin, who tapped his beak on the glass and peered in as if he were looking for me. He returned to this window for another two weeks.

My husband Blair had died suddenly of a brain aneurysm only twenty days earlier. I was awakening from the frozen state of disbelief, still waiting for the garage door to open and hear his cheerful voice announcing, "I'm home!" as he walked in the door. I began to realize my dearest husband was not coming back.

I did not understand why he died so suddenly. But I deliberately trusted in Christ during those lonely months. I knew he was with me. This bird had never appeared before this spring.

I believe one of God's creatures—this cheery, feathered angel—sought me out, letting me know I mattered.

Are you grieving? It could be a death of a loved one. Loss of health. Employment. An estranged relationship. Perhaps you perceive you are no longer useful.

Looking back, I felt the closest to God when in deep grief. He wants you to experience that closeness too. Try reading your Bible. I love reading the Psalms, now and during my times of sorrow. They can even be a prayer when you can't pray. Rest in the comfort of our Savior.

Consider the words of Christ in Matthew 5:4, "Blessed are those who mourn, for they will be comforted." What do those words mean to you? I have come to believe the "blessed" part is the closeness of the presence of God to the person who is grieving.

> What are you grieving today? Write it down below.
> Ask God to help you through this grief.
> Ask him to be present with you during this time.
> Remember, "They will be comforted" (Matthew 5:4).

_____

_____

_____

_____

_____

No Timetable for Grief

Grief is the price of love and grief work the price of healing.
—Shirley Quiring Mozena[11]

The exhausting memorial service was over. It was a wonderful tribute. There had been a huge banner visible when people walked into the worship center, with student notes and drawings. They loved my teacher husband, Blair. I had been surrounded by loving family and friends and felt as though being wrapped in a warm blanket on a snowy day.

The following day was a Sunday, and family members from Florida, Colorado, and Pennsylvania attended church with me. There were many hugs at church with people sharing their condolences. We returned home to a luscious spread of food.

After eating, I said, "I want to watch our wedding video," thinking with this cocoon of family around, it might feel good to relive that beautiful day only seventeen months earlier.

"Are you sure?" My sister asked, her face shadowed with concern.

"Yes." *Why wouldn't I want to watch it?*

My sister, daughter, daughter-in-law, and best friend trooped upstairs to my bedroom. We sat on the king-sized bed, eyes on the screen. I hit the play button on the remote, and suddenly, my very alive husband Blair strode forward on the screen. I gasped in astonishment. There he was, all dressed in his tux, laughing and healthy, anticipating our wedding ceremony. And then, like a splash of cold water thrown in my face, I realized once again he was gone. "Oh. Oh," I wailed. How would I survive this devastation?

Grief is like that. The timetable has good moments tucked in between excruciating agony.

I wept, unconsolably. In a flash, my sisters-in-Christ surrounded me, their arms wrapped tightly around me. Each one prayed out loud for God's strength for me to bear the pain and loss. I felt the soft warmth of their physical bodies, encasing me in their love and care for me along with their own grief. Instantly, I felt the sweet comfort of the Holy Spirit—peace that only comes from him. "My joy has flown away; grief has settled on me. My heart is sick…But I will bring you health and will heal you of your wounds—this is the Lord's declaration" (Jeremiah 8:18; 30:17 HCSB).

Grief is the price of love. When there is loss, pain steps into the void. But there is Someone who will heal you from your wounds of grief. The Lord declares it to be. We can receive that healing. We lean on him during normal times as well as distressing times. He is there, carrying you through. One day, there will be less pain. I can tell you it's true. I am no longer that person so brokenhearted. God healed my pain. Brought me joy with his comfort and presence.

God offers himself. Unwrap the gift of his presence.

Lord, I pray for the person reading this who is grieving the pain of loss. Be with them as they remember their loved one. Heal their wounds. Comfort them. Be with them. In the comforting name of Jesus, amen.

Write on the next page something that
your loved one brought into your life.

Grief with Hope

Love, faithful love, recalled thee to my mind
But how could I forget thee? Through what power,
Even for the least division of an hour,
Have I been so beguiled as to be blind
To my most grievous loss? That thought's return
Was the worst pang that sorrow ever bore,
Save one, one only, when I stood forlorn,
Knowing my heart's best treasure was no more;
That neither present time, nor years unborn
Could to my sight that heavenly face restore.
—"Surprised by Joy—Impatient as the Wind"
by William Wordsworth[12]

Eighteen years ago, I said goodbye to my husband Bill. One of the songs played at the memorial service was by Steven Curtis Chapman, "With Hope." I've rarely listened to that song since the memorial service. Last week, I did. The song reminded me that this wasn't how Bill and I thought our story was supposed to go.

After all those years, listening to the song brought back some of the terrible pain of loss I felt during those days of grief in spite of the happy marriage I am in now.

I know I will see Bill again, but best of all, I'll see the One who made it all possible and gave me the gift of eternal life. We won't ever forget our loved ones, nor do we want to. We treasure the precious memories.

Our tears are laced with hope. "And now, dear brothers and sisters, we want you to know what will happen to the believers who have died so you will not grieve like people who have no hope" (1 Thessalonians 4:13 NLT).

Do you grieve a loved one? Jesus understands your grief more than anyone on earth. "But he said to me, 'My grace is enough for you, for my power is made perfect in weakness'" (2 Corinthians 12:9 NET).

God has never failed his people when they cry out to him. He will not fail you. And he will be your power in weakness.

Father in heaven, you endured much grief
when you witnessed the crucifixion of your Son on the cross.
You gave your Son for our sins. What love!
Thank you for your comfort and grace that is enough.
In your Son's name, Jesus, amen.

Sometimes we haven't completely grieved all of our losses.
List your losses below. Have you worked through each of them?
Say them out loud to God and grieve each loss separately,
asking for God's comfort and guidance.

_____

_____

_____

_____

_____

_____

Take Your Time

*You need to be sure you've worked through your grief
before you even think about marrying again.*
—Second Chance at Love, *by Shirley Quiring Mozena*[13]

Although I had grieved before, I learned that each loss is different. In my loneliness after Blair's death, I became engaged to the wrong person. I stubbornly ignored my unease toward his proposal of marriage. I should have listened to family members who cautioned me I was moving too fast. I should not have pushed doubting thoughts away—doubts that I believe came from the Holy Spirit. Instead, I allowed my hope and strength to come from a man who might make me feel better.

Do you ever pray a prayer you really don't believe God will answer? During my quiet time with God one day, I asked, *Lord, if this marriage is out of your will, you will have to end it, because I cannot.*

That very day, five weeks before our wedding, he broke off our engagement. It was a stinging experience, but I remembered that earlier prayer and recognized that God had answered it.

Once again, I worked through my disappointment and determined to be content in my singleness. Eighteen months passed. I focused on my relationship with God. I volunteered. I traveled. I wrote. I asked God to heal my broken heart. In my singleness, I was comforted by this passage, "I will turn their mourning into joy. I will comfort them and exchange their sorrow for rejoicing" (Jeremiah 31:13 NLT).

I booked a room in a quiet resort for a day and night, licked my wounds, and prayed. I began to understand I hadn't completely recovered from my grief. Instead, I was trying to take away the hurt and loneliness of grief by pursuing a relationship with another man when my grief was not complete. I wasn't ready to date. It wasn't fair to either of us.

After that disaster, I decided to focus on my grief and learn to live alone instead of pursuing a new relationship. I pored through the Bible, asking God to be close to me and heal my broken heart. I traveled alone. Volunteered. Entertained in my home. Finished the book I'd been writing. I led a grief support group. Enjoyed my grandchildren who lived nearby and traveled to those farther away.

Lord, today I pray for the person reading this devotion
who desperately longs to be married.
Help them as they work through their grief.
Be their comfort and sounding board as they wait on you.
You are fully trustworthy. Let them rest in your peace and presence. Amen.

Is there any remaining grief you are working through
before you can move forward with the next thing God has?
Write down the areas of your life
where you've chosen contentment while you wait.
Ask God to show you the next steps to make continued progress.

_____

_____

All Will Be Well

The cost is worth it to be healed and love again.
—Shirley Quiring Mozena[14]

I learned the following to be true: "The Lord is close to the brokenhearted and saves those who are crushed in spirit" (Psalm 34:18). About eighteen months passed after the broken engagement. I began to feel I might be ready for a new relationship. There was still an ache for that special companionship that comes with the right person. But it would also be all right if I stayed single.

I joined a dating service that was new to me. It worked differently, and to sign up you needed to take an extensive personality test. I wrote in my journal, *If this doesn't work, Lord, I won't do any more searching. You will just have to drop him in my lap!* And with a smile, I asked, *Would you make him crazy about me—and love you more than I do?*

Eventually, I began to receive photos and profiles of possible matches. One bright Sunday morning, a new guy came into view. His name was Jim. His profile hinted that he might be a widower. It turns out he was. He gave me a call and asked to meet for coffee. Drinking a cappuccino together, we realized how much our lives paralleled. It wasn't long before we both knew we were right for each other. We married three months later. That was a little over ten years ago.

Jim is a man of character. The more I observe and live with him, the more I admire his qualities. He is loving and kind. He loves his family—and mine, too! Most of all, that last phrase of my prayer was answered, for Jim loves his Father God as much or even more than I do. In God's timing and to my delight, he had answered my prayer.

God does what he promises. He healed my broken heart. Not because I met another man, but because he cares about our broken hearts, concerns himself with our cares and problems. And he can do the same for you. He's right there, waiting for you to ask. God answered that prayer to find my soulmate, and it has been a tremendous gift. But I had to come to a point where I would be content whether or not God would bring someone into my life. In my case, he did. I can't tell you that your prayer for a soulmate will be answered the same way mine was answered, but I can tell you that he will complete the healing process if you let him.

"Create a pure heart in me, O God, and put a new and loyal spirit in me" (Psalm 51:10 GNT). What is most important to you? Your broken heart to be healed—a heart that's disappointed by someone or something? Remarriage? To know God's will for your future—with or without a relationship?

Lately, I've been asking God to reveal my insecurities, to reveal those thoughts that are not good. I pray often, "Create in me a pure heart and renew a steadfast spirit within me" (Psalm 51:10).

Write your own prayer to God below.

_____

_____

_____

Part III

Anchored in
Joy

Forever Peace

*Now may the Lord of peace himself
give you peace at all times and in every way.
The Lord be with all of you.*
—2 Thessalonians 3:16

The child's wispy, nearly white hair rustled in the Nebraska wind as she and her older brother romped among the tombstones one hot, summer afternoon, waiting for their daddy to finish mowing the bumpy cemetery grass. Her brother read the names of the people engraved on the markers. They talked about heaven and how each person needed to ask Jesus to come into their hearts in order to go to heaven. Right there, next to a grave marker, the four-year old girl knelt and prayed to invite Jesus to come into her life. Her brother helped her say the prayer. It most likely was a simple prayer like this: "Dear Jesus, I'm sorry I've been bad sometimes. Please forgive me and come into my heart. I want to be in heaven with you when I die. Amen."

That towheaded girl was me.

The moment I prayed that prayer in the Mennonite cemetery so long ago, the Holy Spirit—God—came into my heart and has been, and still is, cheering me on, gently reminding me when I need to change my attitude and confess wrongdoing. Once we become Christians, we aren't perfect, but we are eternally forgiven, and we need to remember that we have a clean slate with God because of Jesus.

At the point of our conversion—when we confess we are sinners and ask Jesus Christ into our lives—whether we're a child or an adult, we have peace with God. Often, we think of peace as the absence of war or conflict in our emotions or on the earth. But all humans are born with the desperate need and desire for the absence of war and conflict between God and mankind.

At the beginning of time, in the Garden of Eden, there was peace—harmony between Adam and Eve and God. They even met daily with God, walking with him in the cool of the day. Imagine what that would be like—walking and talking with God in paradise.

Jesus came to restore to us the joy of walking and talking with God daily. He lived a pure life with no wrongdoing and became the perfect sacrifice, dying the death that God's law required us to die and rising again to life. Through Adam, sin and death was passed on to all men (Romans 5:12), "but the gift of God is eternal life in Christ Jesus our Lord" (Romans 6:23 ESV).

> *If you declare with your mouth, "Jesus is Lord,"*
> *and believe in your heart that God raised him from the dead,*
> *you will be saved. For it is with your heart that you believe*
> *and are justified, and it is with your mouth*
> *that you profess your faith and are saved.*
> *As Scripture says, "Anyone who believes in him*
> *will never be put to shame."*
> *For there is no difference between Jew and Gentile—*
> *the same Lord is Lord of all and richly blesses all who call on him…*
> *for, "Everyone who calls on the name of the Lord will be saved."*
> —Romans 10:9–11, 13

If you've never acknowledged and turned away from your sin, and you want to walk and talk with your Father daily, acknowledge you are a sinner right now, ask for Jesus's forgiveness, and give your life to him. Your life with Jesus begins right when you do that—here on earth and for eternity. Below is a prayer you can say.

Lord, as I think about your coming to earth
as a perfect human who did not sin,
I thank you for being willing to be our connection to God
through your death and resurrection. Please forgive me for all my sins.
I recognize I've gone my own way. I want you to be my life.
I want you to live through me,
and then I want to live with you in eternity after I die on this earth.
Thank you. In Jesus's name, amen.

Write a prayer of thanks below to God for the joy of your salvation.

_____

_____

_____

_____

_____

_____

_____

_____

A Sacred Cloakroom

For the Kingdom of Heaven belongs to those who are like these children.
—Matthew 19:14 NLT

Thelma's tangled, brown hair hung in strings around her face. Awkwardly, she stomped with uneven steps. She wore a red-and-white checkered blouse, haphazardly tucked into an orange skirt with white flowers. It looked as though her clothes were picked out of a donation barrel. Thelma tried to complete assignments, but she wasn't able to perform her classwork. I don't recall much conversation with her; it seemed she didn't have the ability to communicate. In today's schools, she would have been placed in a special ed classroom, but in the 1950s, all students were bunched together.

Thelma didn't have friends. When I saw her, she was always alone. Sometimes she smelled like she needed a bath. I felt sorry for her and wanted to be a friend to her. Did she know Jesus? I wanted her to have that One who would always be there.

One day, we tugged our boots off after recess in the cloakroom at the back of the classroom. I asked her, "Thelma, do you have Jesus in your heart?"

"I dunno."

"You can ask him if you don't know," I said.

"OK."

"Say this. Dear Jesus." She echoed. After more words, we concluded with "Please come into my heart. Amen."

I don't know what happened to Thelma. I never saw her after the sixth grade, but that day, more than fifty years ago, Thelma's child-like faith, led by another child, is a reminder that "the Kingdom of Heaven belongs to those who are like these children" (Matthew 19:14 NLT). I will meet Thelma again. Whole. Healthy. Bright as all the saints.

Heavenly Father, forgive me for sometimes ignoring people I perceive as unlovely. I know they aren't unlovely to you. Help me see them as you do. In Jesus's name, amen.

Do you remember a Thelma who was a slow, unlovely one in your classroom? Is there a Thelma in your life right now that you can befriend? Does she know Jesus?

Write a plan below and ask God for help in accomplishing it.

_____

_____

_____

_____

_____

_____

_____

He Knows Us

*God's word is alive...and judges the thoughts and feelings in our hearts.
Nothing in all the world can be hidden from God.*
—Hebrews 4:12–13 NCV

It was a school morning. I stepped into my dress and asked to be buttoned up by my mother. "Shirley, you'll have to choose a different dress. You've grown out of it—it's too small." It was my favorite dress, mint green with a bodice that laced up the front—like the picture on the cover of one of my favorite books, *Heidi*. There she was, standing on the slopes of the Alps, wearing a dress just like mine. Right then, I had a tantrum. I cried and stomped into my room to change. It was as though someone else had entered my body, and I couldn't control it. My wise mother allowed me to have my outburst and waited for me to choose another dress. I walked the few blocks to my school and swiped at angry tears.

The day dragged on. I felt sad about and ashamed of my earlier behavior. I knew I'd responded wrong. What made me feel that grief over my temper tantrum? The Holy Spirit living within me. A quiet reminder of whom I belonged to. "And do not grieve the Holy

Spirit of God, with whom you were sealed for the day of redemption" (Ephesians 4:30).

We grieve the Holy Spirit when we let anger control our actions, and the Spirit instructs us how to live and behave: "Do not be bitter or angry or mad. Never shout angrily or say things to hurt others. Never do anything evil. Be kind and loving to each other, and forgive each other just as God forgave you in Christ" (Ephesians 4:31–32 NCV).

At school day's end, I trudged home. Mama greeted me as I walked in the door. I said, "Mama, I'm sorry I had a fit." She took me into her arms, said she forgave me, and gave me a hug—the incident forgotten.

That's what our Savior does to us whenever we confess our wrongdoing to each other. His embrace heals our relationships and our emotions. "Therefore confess your sins to each other and pray for each other so that you may be healed" (James 5:16).

Lord Jesus, help me be the person you want me to be.
Guide my words and thoughts. Help me to be more like you.
In your name, amen.

Write down a short story of something in your past
you need forgiveness for and ask God to forgive you.

_____

_____

_____

_____

_____

_____

Things Can Change

*And we know that in all things God works
for the good of those who love him,
who have been called according to his purpose.*
—Romans 8:28

In the busyness of life as a full-time college student and as a newlywed to my first husband Bill, I lost sight of God in my daily life. I still attended church most Sundays. Bill and I prayed before meals, and if I was desperate about some need, I'd pray.

But then something drastic happened, and God got my attention. When our second baby was born, instead of a lusty cry, the room was silent. The doctor and nurse worked on her for five long minutes before she took her first breath. I didn't get to hold her for three days that seemed like forever.

While waiting to hear if our newborn would be all right, I realized I'd drifted very far from God in spite of attending church and saying those mealtime prayers. So I combed through the Bible. Romans 8:28 gave me comfort.

The doctors were finally able to tell us what was wrong with our infant girl. They told us that just before birth, her blood was transfused back into my body. She was born with only a quarter of her blood. It was a miracle she survived. As a result, they gave her a blood transfusion, and she began to improve almost immediately.

I was so grateful for God's protection of our little one. That was a miracle, but my renewed faith and belief in the God who had been there all along was another miracle. I found a neighborhood Bible study, and the Bible opened up to me as never before. I *wanted* to read and study. Jesus was my best friend. Always there.

What's your story? Once you gave Jesus Christ your life, did you follow him always? I regret those years where I ignored God and went my own way, but after that traumatic birth so long ago, I've never looked back.

Perhaps you've practiced mealtime prayers and even attended church, but you don't have the assurance of knowing Jesus personally or that you'll be in heaven with him after you die. Give him your life today and allow him to transform you into something completely new. Ask Jesus to forgive you for doing things your own way.

Or maybe you began your relationship with Christ a long time ago, but like me, drifted away. Did you put him on a shelf and now only take him down when you need something? Ask for his forgiveness, he's there, waiting for you.

It could be that you are walking in close relationship with him at this very moment, but you want to experience a greater level of intimacy with him.

<blockquote>Wherever you are right now, write a prayer
and listen for his answer.</blockquote>

_____

_____

Things Can Change

Unexpected Protection from God

For he guards the paths of the just and protects those who are faithful to him.
—Proverbs 2:8 NLT

I screamed as the wild lurching of my sporty MG Midget suddenly stopped with me hanging upside down, firmly strapped in my seatbelt. Everything was opposite what it should be. My hand shook as I turned the ignition off. What had happened? I unhooked the seatbelt and tumbled down to the rag top of the car. Just the evening before, my husband had installed a roll bar. I was the designated helper to install it that cold February evening. At last, I had heard the click, click of the ratchet wrench. "OK. All done," he'd announced.

As I pushed the door open and crawled out, nearby voices competed with the *wee-ooo wee*-ooo of an approaching siren. I studied the scene. My MG was flipped upside down in the front yard of a house right next to a telephone pole. The only damage to the car was a broken windshield.

Except for a large bruise on my knee where it was stuck between the steering wheel and door, I was fine.

I had been driving down a backcountry road when barricades had suddenly loomed in front of me. I swerved left and the sensitive steering of the MG jerked the car toward the right, swinging me out of control. If that roll bar not been installed twenty-four hours earlier, if I had hit the telephone pole…wow! A miracle. I could have died.

> *All the days ordained for me were written in your book.*
> —Psalm 139:16

It was not my appointed time. That was God's protection.

What about you? Although we all have experienced moments when we thought God failed us or abandoned us, we have all also experienced countless moments of supernatural protection. Sometimes they aren't as dramatic as my MG accident and are harder to recognize.

Ask God to remind you of the times he protected you in a supernatural way.

> *For he guards the paths of the just and*
> *protects those who are faithful to him.*
> —Proverbs 2:8 NLT

I've learned in the difficult times to thank God and to trust that he knows more than I do about my circumstances. Write your own prayer of thanks below. Share all of your thoughts with him. He understands. And listen to what he says in return.

_____

_____

_____

_____

The Dawn Reveals

*Let the morning bring me word
of your unfailing love,
for I have put my trust in you.
Show me the way I should go,
for to you I entrust my life.*
—Psalm 143:8

I love getting up in the summer. The pearly gray skies awaken me before any alarm. The mornings are pure—no bad news, no conversation, just God's Word on my mind.

One of these mornings, I realized I was resenting someone. Carol had done me wrong, and I was in a funk of un-forgiveness. For months, I'd been grieving over the injustice. As the skies began to turn peachy-pink, I read in Genesis the story of Cain and Abel. Cain was so jealous of Abel's accepted sacrifice that his anger grew until he finally killed his brother (Genesis 4:2–15). Resentment can be like "killing" someone with our mind. I had to do something about this.

As I read more about forgiveness, the Holy Spirit directed me to several passages. "But when you are praying, first forgive anyone you are holding a grudge against, so that your Father in heaven will forgive your sins, too" (Mark 11:25–26 NLT).

There it was in black and white. *Anyone I am holding a grudge against.* There were no exceptions. Not even when I've been wronged. I had to forgive. *Dear Lord,* I prayed, *Please help me forgive Carol. I give my resentments to you. Give me an opportunity to restore the relationship.*

Two weeks later, I attended a conference, and she was there too. While waiting in the buffet line, guess who I stood next to? Carol. I thanked her for all the work she'd done in the contest for our organization. We talked about our dogs, our helpful spouses, and the classes we were taking. The resentment I felt toward her melted like ice cream on a hot day. God had answered my prayer, and the warmth of his love had softened my resentful heart.

God cares about every detail of our lives, including resentment we might be carrying from long ago. It isn't healthy, and it hurts *us*, not the other person.

Thank you, Jesus, for revealing to me again that I must forgive.
Thank You for reminding me. Please help me do this.
I want to obey you, and most of all,
I'm grateful for the forgiveness you gave me when Jesus died for my sins.
In your name, Jesus, amen.

Is there someone you need to forgive? Write a prayer below.

_____

_____

_____

_____

_____

The Bread of Life

Then Jesus declared, "I am the bread of life.
Whoever comes to me will never go hungry,
and whoever believes in me will never be thirsty."
—John 6:35

Mmmmm. My sister and I had just stepped off the school bus, and I could smell the bread my mom was baking from the end of our driveway.

"Can we have a slice of bread?" we begged.

Mom would cut thick pieces of warm bread. We'd slather them with honey or jam and enjoy them, sometimes with the sticky honey running between our fingers. The after-school snack helped curb hunger after a long day at school.

Bread is considered a basic dietary food. Every culture has some type of bread, from pita to focaccia to flatbread to chapati to cornbread. Bread was part of the Passover meal. The Jews were fed manna—bread from heaven—during their years of wandering in the desert. And in the New Testament, a boy gave his five small loaves of bread and two fish to Jesus, who made the lunch feed a multitude of hungry people.

Jesus was bold enough to say he was everything essential for life. He didn't mean physical life but spiritual life. He claimed he was divine by saying he was the Bread of Life. Notice he says in John 6:35 that we must "come" to him and "believe." This is an invitation for those listening or reading to place their faith in Jesus and believe that he is who he says he is. He promises that those who come to him will never be hungry or thirsty again—not physical hunger or thirst but the hunger and thirst to be made righteous in the sight of God.[15] He is our everything when we believe in him.

Lord, I celebrate your presence in my life.
Thank you for providing everything I need in you.
I believe you are God who came to earth as our Savior.
You provided for us by being the perfect sacrifice on the cross.
You rose again and you give us eternal life when we believe.
Thank you for being my Bread of Life.

Write a situation that you are especially thankful to God for and write a prayer, thanking him.

_____

_____

_____

_____

_____

_____

_____

Someone Safe, Someone Good

Then shall my every breath
Sing out Your praise;
This be the only song
My heart shall raise;
This still my prayer shall be:
More love, O Christ, to Thee
More love to Thee,
More love to Thee!
—"More Love to Thee" Elizabeth Prentiss (1818–1878)[16]

I feel very safe with my husband Jim. We talk about many subjects, and he is my closest friend. But there is One who knows me even deeper than my wonderful husband. One who knows those deep secrets you tell no one. And in spite of those rotten, unwanted, embarrassing thoughts, God knows.

Psalm 139 reminds us, "O Lord, you have examined my heart and know everything about me. You know when I sit down or stand up. You know my thoughts even when I'm far away" (vv. 1–2). The psalmist goes on, revealing even more about us: "You saw me before I was born. Every day of my life was recorded in your book. Every moment was laid out before a single day had passed. How precious are your thoughts about me, O God. They cannot be numbered! I can't even count them; they outnumber the grains of sand! And when I wake up, you are still with me!" (vv. 16–18).

God knows everything about us and loves us. We are precious. Precious means "of high price or great value; very valuable or costly." That is astounding to me. He knows everything about me. He knows even how many days I will live.

Thank you, heavenly Father for being the safe One I can always approach, just as I am. I want to love you more. In Jesus's name, amen.

Write a prayer of thanks to God for his incredible love for you below.

_____

_____

_____

_____

_____

_____

_____

_____

_____

_____

Give the Blessing

Great is Thy Faithfulness, O God my Father,
There is no shadow of turning with Thee;
Thou changest not,
Thy compassions they fail not
As Thou hast been, Thou forever wilt be.
—Thomas O. Chisholm[17]

When I was in my early teens, I loved to wander in a cemetery near my home. I enjoyed the sun-dappled place where I could read the names on tipped headstones more than a hundred years old, some with an epitaph on them. I wondered who these people were and what their lives had been like.

A few years ago, I read in the Old Testament that patriarchs would give a blessing to their family members when they were approaching the end of their lives. I felt compelled to give a blessing to my two children. So I wrote both of them a letter reflecting on God's goodness upon my life—and their lives too. I included my hopes for them to follow God as well.

The book of Psalms reminds us, "Teach us to number our days, that we may gain a heart of wisdom" (Psalm 90:12).

All of us are born to die. Each day brings us closer to our time to enter eternity. I have experienced enough deaths to know one shouldn't wait to tell another certain truths. Sometimes it's simply "I love you," "You did well," or "I'm so glad God gave you to me."

I still visit that cemetery I wandered through many years ago. There are family members who now lie there.

One day, there will be a marker with my name on it. The longer I live, the more aware I am of the faithfulness of God. He reminds me each morning when I wake up.

The faithful love of the Lord never ends!
His mercies never cease.
Great is his faithfulness;
his mercies begin afresh each morning.
—Lamentations 3:22–23 NLT

Thank you, Lord, for the days appointed for me.
Help me remember your mercies every morning. Amen.

How has God been faithful to you? Write those experiences down. Do you need to write a blessing to someone? Why not do it today?

_____

_____

_____

_____

_____

_____

Give the Blessing

Want to Meet for Coffee?

Questions flew between the two.
Did she love Jesus, did he?
Aha, want to meet for coffee?
Bingo, the match seemed a coup!
—Judi Mayfield, 2013

Jim talked openly of his faith in Jesus Christ. He spoke of his desire to be an influence of faith to friends and family. That was huge to me—more important than anything else. He talked about his interest in keeping his body in shape by regularly running the hills near his home. I liked that. Keeping in good physical condition was important to me too.

We met for a coffee date that lasted two hours. Over cappuccinos, we learned more about each other and found we had so much in common. There was another date and then another. One cool fall morning, Jim took me to a former rock quarry turned into a beautiful place of prayer. There, beneath a statue of Jesus, he knelt on one knee and asked, "Shirley Quiring Rudberg Graybill, will you marry me?"

Without a doubt in my mind, I said, "Yes."

We married three months later on a frosty December morning.

Sometimes people ask us, "Do you love your present wife/husband as much as you did your late spouses?"

I like Jim's analysis of his love for me. He describes his love like an urn made of pottery. When he married his wife Kathy, he loved her with everything he could. The urn was full.

Then during the trials of raising a family, facing the death of their daughter, and the deadly Pulmonary Fibrosis that took her life, Jim's love filled the urn to the brim. After she died, the urn seemed like it was scrubbed by grief and loss and stretched even larger.

When Jim met me, his vessel had grown. He had the capacity to love me even more. Not that his love for Kathy was less, he gave her all the love he had the capacity to give. Now his vessel was larger and had a greater capacity to love.

And I pray that you, being rooted and established in love,
may have power, together with all the Lord's holy people,
to grasp how wide and long and high and deep is the love of Christ,
and to know this love that surpasses knowledge—
that you may be filled to the measure of all the fullness of God.
—Ephesians 3:17–19

Dear reader, do you realize how much Jesus Christ loves you?
Meditate on Ephesians 3:17–19. Ask God to show you
how wide and long and high and deep Christ loves you.
Write a prayer to God below.
Thank him for his love that surpasses knowledge.

_____

_____

_____

Want to Meet for Coffee?

We're Standing on Their Shoulders

*Grow old along with me! The best is yet to be, the last of life,
for which the first was made.
Our times are in his hand...Trust God:
See all, nor be afraid!*
—Robert Browning[18]

My husband Jim and I often say, "We're standing on the shoulders of our previous spouses," because our previous marriages have benefited our present marriage. Although not perfect, our marriage is as close to perfection as life can be on this planet.

We both realize that our most important relationship is with our Savior, Jesus Christ. This is the most permanent relationship you will ever have. Our vertical relationship with God outshines and deserves the most attention. It lasts through eternity.

Although we love our spouses here on earth, marital love is temporary. "For in the resurrection there is no such thing as marrying or being given in marriage" (Matthew 22:30 PHILLIPS). Marriage is a gift from God for us to enjoy here. "God gives the lonely a home" (Psalm 68:6 NCV).

Just this past December, we celebrated ten years together. We are grateful for our second chance at love and can say with full assurance we're delighted we met and married.

I don't know the future, but I know I can trust my Savior. He brought me through the very hard times I've experienced. He is with me in the joyful times too. He is with me when I celebrate birthdays or anniversaries, when I travel with my Jim, when we have new adventures, and when we make love.

Sometimes there are niggles of fear that creep into my thoughts. *What if Jim dies? Can I make it without his love and care?*

We pray that God will grant us many years together, but we know that our lives are truly in his hands, not ours. We can trust in the God who loves us more than we love each other.

So we do just that. We trust.

And he'll be there when he takes each of us home to him.

Father God, thank you for inventing marriage with the first couple and smiling on marriages here on earth. We benefit from each other and the strength we give each other through marriage.
Help us to honor our marriages and treat them as a precious gift.
In Jesus's name, amen.

Write a prayer of thanks
for the positive aspects of your marriage—past or present.

_____

_____

_____

_____

_____

Look to the East

Be strong and courageous, and do the work.
Don't be afraid or discouraged, for the Lord God, my God, is with you.
He will not fail you or forsake you.
He will see to it that all the work related to the Temple of the Lord
is finished correctly.
—1 Chronicles 28:20 NLT

"Congratulations, you're at the top. Now turn around; we're going back down!" It was my first mountain climb of the highest peak in Oregon—Mt. Hood. After finishing the climb in whiteout conditions, my husband Bill and I couldn't see a thing. Our climb leader told us we were there, so we trusted it was so.

After the climb, our group along with our leaders, stopped at a local restaurant nearby and celebrated with pie and coffee, heady with the wonderful experience of accomplishing something that was difficult.

We climbed many more mountains after that, and the best part of it all was the bonding of our relationship.

I no longer climb mountains, but this morning while preparing to write the final devotional for this book, I read 1 Chronicles 28:20:

"Be strong and courageous, and do the work." It was like an audible voice telling me to turn around and "climb back down," celebrating the completion of this goal and preparing for the next.

As the years pass, I often wonder what my next task will be. Some of my friends are gone now, and I'm not sure how much longer I will be here on earth. But while I am able, I will spend time at my desk, crafting words of encouragement, waiting to hear from God, knowing he is with me.

A Japanese proverb says: "We can never see the sunrise by looking west." My desk is situated right by a window that faces east. Most mornings, I am up before the sunrise, and when I see the sky lighten, I am encouraged with the new day.

What is your work?
Do you sometimes feel it's like the silly hamster
who spins for hours on his wheel?
Or do you wake up each day inspired with purpose and providence?
Write what God is speaking to you about your next task below.

_____

_____

_____

_____

_____

_____

_____

Endnotes

1. Public Domain: *We Have an Anchor* (The New Church Hymnal) WORDS: Priscilla J. Owens, 1907, MUSIC: William J. Kirkpatrick, 1921.

2. Poetry.com, STANDS4 LLC, 2024. "Obedience" by George MacDonald. Accessed May 13, 2024. https://www.poetry.com/poem/42956/obedience.

3. Got Questions. 2023. "What does it mean that 'my sheep hear my voice' (John 10:27)?" Last updated January 30, 2023. https://www.gotquestions.org/my-sheep-hear-my-voice.html.

4. https://theweddingprojectphilippinessite.wordpress.com/2017/09/09/our-top-10-quote-about-love-and-marriage/

5. Timeless Truths. n.d. "Quiet Rest" by Cleland McAfee, 1903. Accessed May 13, 2024. https://library.timelesstruths.org/music/Near_to_the_Heart_of_God/.

6. Hymnary.org. n.d. "Hark the Glad Sound! The Saviour Comes" by Philip Doddridge, 1735. Accessed May 13, 2024. https://hymnary.org/text/hark_the_glad_sound_the_savior_comes.

7. Doddridge, Philip, "Hark the Glad Sound! The Saviour Comes," 1735. https://hymnary.org/text/hark_the_glad_sound_the_savior_comes.

8. Miller, James, *Winter Grief, Summer Grace: Returning to Life After a Loved One Dies*. Augsburg Fortress, 1995.

9. Sandell, Carolina, "Day by Day," 1865, The New Church Hymnal, p. 334, LEXICON MUSIC, INC., 1976.

10. Mozena, Shirley Quiring. 2023. "It's for You!" Last modified April 21, 2023. https://shirleymozena.com/spiritual-reflections/its-for-you.

11. Mozena, Shirley Quiring, *Second Chance at Love: A Practical Guide to Remarriage after Loss*. SCM Publishing, 2023.

12. Public Domain Poetry. n.d. "Surprised by Joy - Impatient as the Wind" by William Wordsworth. Accessed May 13, 2024. https://www.public-domain-poetry.com/william-wordsworth/surprised-by-joy-impatient-as-the-wind-3892.

13. Mozena, Shirley Quiring, *Second Chance at Love: A Practical Guide to Remarriage after Loss*, p. 33. SCM Publishing, 2023.

14. Mozena, Shirley Quiring, *Second Chance at Love: A Practical Guide to Remarriage after Loss*, p. 40. SCM Publishing, 2023.

15. Got Questions. 2022. "What did Jesus mean when He said, "I am the Bread of Life" (John 6:35)?" Last updated January 24, 2022. https://www.gotquestions.org/bread-of-life.html.

16. PUBLIC DOMAIN: *More Love to Thee* (The New Church Hymnal 299), WORDS: Elizabeth Prentiss, MUSIC: W.H. Doane.

17. Chisholm, Thomas, "Great is Thy Faithfulness," 1923, The New Church Hymnal, p. 196, LEXICON MUSIC, INC., 1976.

18. Goodreads. n.d. "Robert Browning > Quotes > Quotable Quote." Accessed May 13, 2024. https://www.goodreads.com/quotes/71023-grow-old-along-with-me-the-best-is-yet-to

Acknowledgments

I want to thank my husband, Jim Mozena, best friend and greatest cheerleader. He carefully listened to my ideas, reading the devotions numerous times and giving helpful suggestions to them.

To the many people who gave me encouragement, hope, and strength during the storms of life. Without them, I wouldn't have any stories to tell. Thanks especially to my Vancouver Christian Writers' group as well as the online Camas Scribes group for their helpful input.

I am also grateful for my editor, Rachel Bradley at Revisions by Rachel. Rachel was always thoughtful and gave constructive comments with each of my articles.

As well, I'm grateful for those pastors throughout my life, counselors, GriefShare facilitators, friends and family, too numerous to mention individually.

About the Author

SHIRLEY QUIRING MOZENA, author of three books—*Second Chances at Life and Love with Hope, Beyond Second Chances: Heartbreak to Joy,* and *Second Chance at Love: A Practical Guide to Remarriage after Loss*—is a retreat speaker and, for the past eleven years, a national speaker for Stonecroft Ministries. She has hundreds of followers who read her weekly blog on encouragement, grief, and hope. She has a presence on Facebook, LinkedIn, and Instagram.

Shirley has published articles in her local newspaper, Christian publications, and in "Angels on Earth" magazine. She was three times a finalist in the Cascade Christian Writers (CCW) Cascade Awards for her books. *Second Chance at Love* was also a finalist in the 2021 Selah Awards and in 2024 for the Next Generation Indie Book Awards.

She has a heart for those grieving the loss of loved ones in death and helping them work through their loss to the other side of grief. With her husband, Jim, she facilitates GriefShare in their church.

Shirley has piloted an airplane, climbed many of the mountain peaks in the Pacific Northwest, was a rock climber, and hiked many trails in the PNW. She enjoys mentoring young women and leading women's Bible studies. She lives in Washington State and enjoys walking in her neighborhood with her husband, Jim, and plucky Yorky terrier, Rudy.

Connect with Shirley

Website: ShirleyMozena.com

Email: Shirley@ShirleyMozena.com

∿

May you be inspired and stirred

to seek Jesus Christ in everything you do.

He is there!

∿

Other Books by Shirley

Second Chance at Love: A Practical Guide to Remarriage after Loss

Whether your marriage was blissful or challenging, lengthy or short, it didn't end the way you imagined. Regardless of how you found yourself without a life partner, you may be at a point where you'd like to experience the love of a spouse again. Authors Shirley and Jim Mozena experienced devastating losses and then struggles in their relationships before finding renewed love with each other, and in Second Chance at Love they offer their insights to these difficult questions:

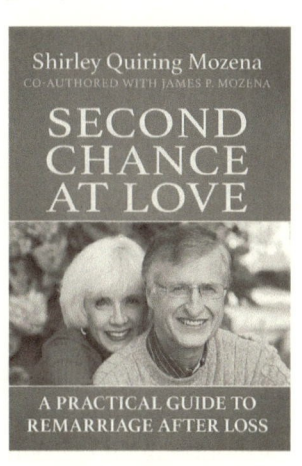

- Are you really ready?
- Is now the time?
- How do you know if you've found the right one?
- Is the potential pain of losing another spouse worth it?

The authors approach their answers with practical reality and their own vulnerability. They share the experiences of their first marriages, their second marriages, their journeys through what seemed like devastating losses, and the gifts of finding love and another chance to share their lives with a spouse after death and divorce.

In addition to the down-to-earth guidance on the situations you face when considering marrying again, Shirley and Jim have created valuable questionnaires to identify issues and facilitate discussions with potential mates. The information contained in this book will give you confidence and peace as you navigate these hopeful waters.

Second Chance at Love: A Practical Guide to Remarriage after Loss **is available at Shirley's website (shirleymozena.com) or on amazon.com and barnesandnoble.com**

Second Chances at Life and Love, with Hope

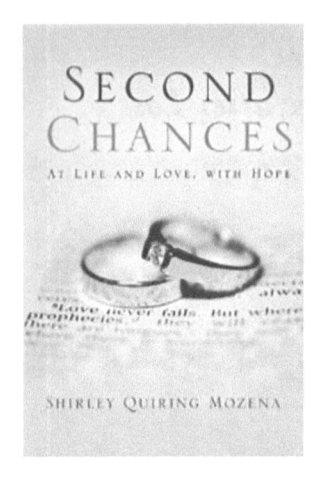

When Shirley and Bill set out on a dream trip in the beautiful northwest wilderness to celebrate their 40th anniversary, what develops is a nightmare that has no end. Mysterious pangs turn into a vicious virus that makes its way into Bill's body. Shirley finds comfort through her Savior during the six months of Bill's illness—an illness which eventually takes his life.

After a time, Shirley's heart aches for companionship. Little does she know that living a few miles from her home, a widower mourns the loss of his wife of 32 years. They meet and fall hopelessly in love, and their love takes them on a two-year journey of joy and adventure until once again overwhelming heartbreak rocks Shirley's world. This is a story of faith and courtship to strengthen your own soul.

Praise for *Second Chances*:

This story is wonderfully written with honesty and the depth of understanding that only grief can bring. In spite of the sad story of loss, the message of the book is one of joy in the goodness of today and hope for a future with God.

—**Jan Pierce**, author

Be ready for an "all-nighter" once you open this book. Shirley shares her times of love, sorrow, joy, peace and renewal. Shirley's willingness to open her heart to help others is seen throughout the book.

—**Judi Mayfield**, author

I just finished reading Second Chances. *Thank you for sharing your story with authenticity and candor… your trust in our kind Father has been your bedrock…*

—**Diane Stevens**

Second Chances is available at Shirley's website (shirleymozena.com) or on amazon.com and barnesandnoble.com

Beyond Second Chances

The true story of a woman, twice widowed, who finds fulfilling love again. After grappling with loneliness, Shirley enters a hasty courtship, and is crushed by a broken engagement just before the wedding. Once again, Shirley's dreams have been destroyed. In her grief, she fully surrenders to God, faces her challenges and learns to trust Him more deeply.

Praise for *Beyond Second Chances*:
I just finished your book and wish so much that I had read it BEFORE meeting you and Jim in Branson at Hope Restored. You are both living proof that our generous God does restore hope, because He loves us so personally.

—**Rona**, Colorado Springs, CO

Beyond Second Chances **is available at Shirley's website (shirleymozena.com) or on amazon.com and barnesandnoble.com**

Made in United States
Troutdale, OR
09/22/2024

23040046R00094